Famous Men
of the 16th and 17th
Century

by Robert G. Shearer

Greenleaf Press
Lebanon, Tennessee

To Cyndy and the children
my life's greatest adventure

©Robert G. Shearer, 2009
Published by Greenleaf Press, Lebanon, Tennessee

Internet: www.greenleafpress.com
3761 Highway 109N, Unit D
Lebanon, Tennessee 37087
615-449-1617

GReenleaf
P·R·E·S·S

Table of Contents

Introduction

For the first half of the 16th century, students should read **Famous Men of the Renaissance & Reformation** (which covers the period from roughly 1350 to 1550). This volume begins with the first generation after the Reformation and the two key figures in England and France. I have chosen to begin with **Catherine de' Medici,** (Queen of France from 1536-1559; then Regent & Queen Mother from 1559-1589) and **Elizabeth I** of England (whose reign began in 1559). These two powerful (and politically skillful) women dominated European dynastic and political affairs for most of the period from 1550 to 1600. And yes, I am aware of the irony of beginning a book titled Famous *Men* with the biographies of two women. My hope is that the choice of Elizabeth and Catherine will provide confirmation of my assertion that the use of the phrase "Famous Men" has all along been intended in the generic, inclusive sense. My selection of figures ends with the life of **Louis XIV,** the Sun King, whose reign defined France from 1650 to his death in 1715.

The eleven chapters on *Henry of Navarre, Sir Francis Drake, Sir Walter Raleigh, Gustavus Adophus, Wallenstein, Galileo, Richelieu, Cromwell, Jan Sobieski, William of Orange*, and *Louis XIV* were all originally published in **Famous Men of Modern Times** by John Haaren and A.B. Poland in 1909. I have taken the liberty of editing (and in some cases, completely re-writing) their work in order to bring it up to date with more recent scholarship and to adapt it to fit with the other 17 chapters in this work.

The Seventeenth Century has been unjustly overlooked in the history books. It was a critical time in the political and intellectual development of the modern world. Textbooks, and most survey courses, seem anxious to race from the Reformation to the French Revolution (only lightly touching on The Armada, Shakespeare and the Pilgrims). Only the English historians, because of the importance of the English civil war, have paid much attention to this period, and often their perspective is parochial and stops at the English Channel. The American historians are worse, seeming to assume that the world began in 1492 and skipping quickly through to the

Pilgrims and then rapidly on to George Washington. Jamestown is mostly ignored, because, after all, the South lost the Civil War. It is the best of times, it is the worst of times. The teaching of history has fallen into neglect and disfavor. At the same time, there have been a number of new works of scholarship that have taken thoughtful, balanced, more sophisticated approaches. I have benefited immensely from recent works of scholarship on Bradford and Winthrop by Schmidt and Bremer which have sought to set them firmly in the context of the political and religious developments in their native England. My ability to gather information about the other 28 figures has been enhanced both by recent scholarship and by the increased ease of access to original source material made possible by the internet.

My plan is to follow this volume with three more: **Famous Men of the 18th Century**, **Famous Men of the 19th Century**, and **Famous Men of the 20th Century**. When they are all completed, Greenleaf will have published four books on the ancient world (Israel, Egypt, Greece, & Rome), two on the Middle Ages, Renaissance, and Reformation, and four on modern times. These will form the backbone of an introduction to the history of Western Civilization suitable for students in grades K-12.

My experience in researching, and writing these biographies has confirmed the wisdom of Wordsworth's line, "the child is father to the man." Again and again, as I reviewed and selected details of each biography to retell, I was struck by how much each of these historical figures were shaped by their childhood experiences, especially their experience of father, mother, and siblings. It is, I believe, impossible to understand or make sense of these figures as adults unless you know what kind of childhood, upbringing, and education they had. And so, each of these biographies is weighted towards providing as much of the story of their youth as I could find out.

- Rob Shearer, August 2, 2009

The Medici
The Last of the Valois Kings
The Bourbon Kings

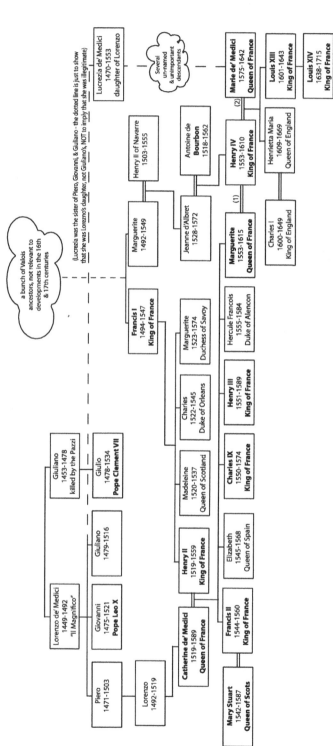

a bunch of Valois ancestors, not relevant to developments in the 16th & 17th centuries

Several un-named & unimportant descendants

(Lucrezia was the sister of Piero, Giovanni, & Giuliano - the dotted line is just to show that she was Lorenzo's daughter, not Giuliano's daughter; not Giuliano's, NOT to imply that she was illegitimate)

Lorenzo de' Medici
1449-1492
"Il Magnifico"

Giuliano
1453-1478
killed by the Pazzi

Giulio
1478-1534
Pope Clement VII

Lucrezia de' Medici
1470-1553
daughter of Lorenzo

Piero
1471-1503

Giovanni
1475-1521
Pope Leo X

Giuliano
1479-1516

Lorenzo
1492-1519

Henry II
1519-1559
King of France

Catherine de' Medici
1519-1589
Queen of France

Madeleine
1520-1537
Queen of Scotland

Charles
1522-1545
Duke of Orleans

Marguerite
1523-1574
Duchess of Savoy

Francis I
1494-1547
King of France

Henry II of Navarre
1503-1555

Marguerite
1492-1549

Francis II
1544-1560
King of France

Mary Stuart
1542-1587
Queen of Scots

Elizabeth
1545-1568
Queen of Spain

Charles IX
1550-1574
King of France

Henry III
1551-1589
King of France

Hercule Francois
1555-1584
Duke of Alencon

Antoine de Bourbon
1518-1562

Jeanne d'Albret
1528-1572

Marguerite
1553-1615
Queen of France

(1)

Henry IV
1553-1610
King of France

(2)

Marie de' Medici
1575-1642
Queen of France

Charles I
1600-1649
King of England

Henrietta Maria
1609-1669
Queen of England

Louis XIII
1601-1643
King of France

Louis XIV
1638-1715
King of France

Louis
1661-1711
le Grand Dauphin

Louis
1682-1712
Duke of Burgundy

Louis XV
1710-1774
King of France

Catherine de' Medici

Background

In 1519, Cortez, the great Spanish conquistador, led a small band of mercenary adventurers in the conquest of the Aztec Empire in Mexico.

In Europe, the young Habsburg prince from Burgundy, Charles, already King of Spain by inheritance from his mother's parents, Ferdinand & Isabella, was elected **Holy Roman Emperor.**

All over the Empire (and also in France, England, & Italy) Martin Luther's writings on the scandal of indulgences were being widely printed and read. Pope Leo X, irritated and annoyed, was on the brink of excommunicating him.

In Florence, a baby girl named Catherine was born – a new princess in the famous Medici family. Her father, just 27 years old, was Lorenzo II, grandson of Lorenzo the Magnificent, and nephew to the pope. Her mother was a beautiful 17-year-old French aristocrat, Madeleine de la Tour d'Auvergne, Countess of Boulogne. Lorenzo and Madeleine had been married for just a little over a year. A month after the birth of their daughter Catherine, both Lorenzo and Madeleine were dead of the plague.

After the death of her parents, Catherine spent the first eight years of her life growing up in Florence, cared for by her aunts. When her great-uncle, Pope Leo X (Giovanni de' Medici), died, Cardinal Giulio de' Medici became the head of the Medici family. He was elected Pope Clement VII in 1524. In 1527, the Medici were overthrown in Florence by a popular uprising supported by the rivals of Pope Clement VII. The eight-year-old Catherine was taken hostage and placed in a series of convents. After three anxious years, Pope Clement, with the help of the Emperor Charles V, defeated his rivals and once again Florence was ruled by the Medici. The eleven-year-old Catherine was brought from the convent in Florence to live with her much older cousin, Pope Clement, in Rome.

When she was fourteen, Pope Clement arranged for her marriage to Prince Henry, Duke of Orleans, the second son of King Francis I of France. Two years later, Prince Henry's older brother, Francois, caught a chill after a game of tennis, contracted a fever, and died. Catherine's husband, Prince Henry, was now the heir to the kingdom of France.

In 1547, King Francis I, died. Henry and Catherine (both 28 years old), became King and Queen of France.

The France that Henry and Catherine ruled over was bitterly divided over matters of religion. In 1536, a French scholar, Jean Cauvin (John Calvin), had written an admirable summary of the protestant faith (**The Institutes of Christian Religion**). He dedicated the treatise to King Francis I (Catherine's father-in-law) with an appeal to the King to reform the French church. Francis rejected the appeal and ordered Protestants arrested as heretics. Calvin fled France and settled in Geneva. There he continued to write, preach, and teach French Protestants (also known as Huguenots) who returned to France to lead secret, underground churches.

Catherine de' Medici

King Henry II of France

When Henry became King in 1547, he vowed to rid France of all heretics. He instructed his officials to arrest and punish them, particularly their ministers. The punishment was often burning at the stake or having their tongues cut off for speaking heresies. Even those merely suspected of being Protestants could be imprisoned. The Edict of Chateaubriand (27 June 1551) called upon the civil and ecclesiastical courts to detect and punish all heretics. The Edict also prohibited the sale, importation, or printing of any unapproved book.

It didn't work. In spite of the persecution by the King the number of Protestants continued to grow.

Henry and Catherine's family also grew. They had had one son, Francis, before becoming King and Queen. Now they had three more sons (Charles, Henry, & Hercules) and three daughters (Elizabeth, Claude, & Margaret).

After 12 years as King and Queen, Henry and Catherine, each now 40 years old, were in the prime of life. In April of 1559 King Henry II signed a peace treaty with the Holy Roman Empire which brought to an end fifty years of war between the Valois Kings of France and the Habsburg Emperors of Germany (and Kings of Spain). As a part of the treaty, Henry and Catherine betrothed their daughter Elizabeth to King Philip II of Spain. King Philip II (then 32 years old) had been widowed the previous year when his wife, Queen Mary I of England, had died.

There was peace, and there was going to be a wedding. The wedding, in June of 1559, was celebrated with festivities, balls, masques, and five days of jousting. King Henry II took part in the jousting himself. He won his first two matches, but in the third match a young French knight, Gabriel, the Count de Montgomery, a member of the king's Scottish guard, shattered his lance against the helmet of the King. One of the splinters pierced the king's eye and entered his brain. He died ten days later.

Catherine was devastated. From that day on, until she died, she wore black in mourning for her husband.

King Francis II of France

Henry and Catherine's eldest son became King Francis II at the age of 15. Catherine looked forward to watching him rule as king and assisting him from the background. But this was not to be. Seventeen months after becoming King, Francis II died of an ear infection just before his seventeenth birthday.

King Charles IX of France

Catherine's next son, Charles, only nine years old, now became King Charles IX of France. Catherine could not stand in the background. She decided she must rule as regent, in her son's name, and keep France strong until he was old enough to rule on his own.

The biggest problem facing France continued to be the religious division between Catholic and Protestant. The majority of the country had remained Catholic, but there was a significant minority who had embraced the Protestant faith, including a number of influential nobles.

Catherine decided to call for a conference between the bishops of the Catholic Church in France and the leaders of the Huguenots. Six French cardinals and 38 archbishops and bishops attended the conference, held in a convent at Poissy, just outside Paris in September of 1561. The Huguenot delegation was led by Theodore Beza, Calvin's successor in Geneva. Catherine was actively involved in the proceedings and wished desperately for some agreement which all French Christians could agree to. But the differences between the two sides were too great. After a month of meetings, the conference broke up without any agreement.

Six months later came a shocking incident that triggered 36 years of civil war. In March of 1562, one of the great nobles of France, François, the Duke of Guise, travelling with his troops to his estates, stopped in Vassy and decided to attend Mass. In the town, he found a congregation of Huguenots holding religious services. Outraged, he ordered their minister to stop. The Huguenots, outraged in turn by this rude interruption of their worship, began to throw stones at the Duke. His men then opened fire. When the shooting stopped, over sixty of the Huguenots had been killed and more than two hundred wounded.

The Massacre at Vassy began a civil war between Catholics and Protestants. The Protestants (or Huguenots) were led by a veteran soldier and nobleman, Gaspard de Coligny. He

was joined by the young Henry of Navarre. The Catholic party was led by Henry, Duke of Guise –
who was the son of that Francois, Duke of Guise who had been responsible for the Massacre at
Vassy. Francois had been ambushed and shot outside the city of Orleans by a Protestant soldier.

In 1570, Catherine and her son King Charles realized that eight years of war had
accomplished nothing. The kingdom was practically bankrupt and Catherine advised Charles that
they must sign a treaty of peace with the Huguenots. The King agreed to allow the Huguenots
the liberty to establish their own churches and to worship as they pleased everywhere in France,
except the city of Paris. The Huguenots were allowed to keep control of four strong cities and to
maintain a garrison of soldiers in each of them as a safeguard against any future conflict. Finally,
the Peace of St. Germain proclaimed a general pardon to all who had taken up arms against the
king.

Henry of Guise was not happy with the Peace of St. Germain.
The Protestants were heretics and had been responsible for the death
of his father. He thought that Catherine and King Charles should have
continued the war until the Huguenots were defeated and forced to
repent of their errors, or sent into exile. When Catherine announced
that her youngest daughter Marguerite would marry the Huguenot
Henry of Navarre, Henry of Guise left the court in anger and disgust.
Both the Pope and King Philip of Spain condemned Catherine for her
decision to arrange a marriage between her daughter and a Protestant
heretic.

Henry, Duke of Guise

In August of 1572, the marriage of Marguerite of Valois, and Henry of Navarre took
place just outside the cathedral of Notre Dame. The wedding could not take place inside the
church, because Henry was not a catholic. Many of the Huguenot leaders had come to Paris to
help celebrate the wedding. They hoped that this marriage would bring the wars of religion in
France to an end.

Three days after the wedding, the veteran soldier Gaspard de Coligny, leader of the Huguenots, was walking back to his rooms from the royal palace when a shot rang out from a house and wounded him in the hand and arm. Coligny was carried back to his rooms, but his physicians soon determined that the wounds were not serious, and he was expected to recover quickly.

It is not clear if Catherine was responsible for the plot to assassinate Coligny. The Guise family were certainly behind it. They may have been supported and assisted by the King of Spain. There is some evidence that Catherine knew about the plot, but did nothing to stop it.

But Catherine was involved in what happened next. She and her son, King Charles IX met to discuss what they should do. The Huguenots were angry and demanding vengeance for the attack on Coligny. The Guise family were angry and wanted to end all toleration for the Protestant heretics. Catherine and Charles made a fateful decision. They would take advantage of the fact that all the Huguenot leaders were still in Paris for the wedding of Henry of Navarre. They would have them all arrested and executed.

The King's personal guard were given a list of leading Protestants who were to be killed. The signal to begin would be the ringing of the church bells for matins, which occurred early in the morning, shortly after midnight – on the feast of St. Bartholomew.

Catherine brought the Guise family into the plot. When the bells rang, Henry, Duke of Guise was directed to personally supervise the capture and execution of Gaspard de Coligny.

Catherine dispatched further orders to the commander of the militia in Paris to close the city gates and guard all entrances & exits from the city. She also gave orders that her new son-in-law, Henry of Navarre (and his cousin, the Prince de Conde) were to be spared – though their companions should be killed.

Catherine believed perhaps that by killing a hundred or so of the leading Huguenots, she could protect her son the King and remove the threat to his reign by these rebellious heretics. But her terrible decision led quickly to a massacre that killed thousands.

Gaspard de Coligny was killed first. Just after midnight, as the bells rang, the Duke of Guise and his followers arrived at his hotel, broke down the door and trapped him in his rooms on the second floor. He was stabbed repeatedly, and then his body hurled from a second story window into the street where Duke Henry stood waiting. Then the king's guards began to hunt down the Huguenot nobles in the palace. Henry of Navarre was separated from his followers and friends, and locked in a room. His companions were slaughtered. Not just the men were executed, but entire families of Huguenots perished, including women and children. By dawn there was a large pile of corpses in the courtyard of the Louvre.

Catherine de' Medici views the aftermath of the St. Bartholomew's Day massacre

The violence quickly spread beyond the attacks on the visiting Huguenot nobles. The militia of Paris began systematically killing Protestants throughout the city. They were joined by large crowds of citizens who attacked the homes of Protestants, drug the terrified inhabitants into the streets, and killed them all. For three days, the killing continued. When it was over, at least 3,000 Protestants had been killed in Paris.

The killing also spread to the other cities and provinces of France. No one, to this day knows how many were killed, but it was certainly many times the number who perished in Paris.

Protestants outside France were outraged and aghast. Queen Elizabeth of England was concerned that the actions of the King of France might be the beginning of a plot to kill Protestants all over Europe.

In France, civil war broke out again. The Huguenots were besieged in their chief cities of Sommieres and La Rochelle. For a year the siege continued, but neither side could gain an advantage. Finally, a truce was signed. The exhausted Huguenots were forced to give up their right to have their own churches. They were now restricted to worshipping publicly only in La Rochelle and two other smaller cities. But Catherine and Charles agreed that they were otherwise to be left alone.

Henry of Valois
King Henry III of France

Within a few months however, King Charles IX, never strong, weakened and died. He was only 23. He had been king for thirteen years. During most of his reign, Catherine de' Medici had been the real power in France. She had controlled the king's council. She had issued the orders which had gone out in his name. Even when he was declared old enough to rule on his own, she continued to control the kingdom.

Catherine had now buried a husband, and two of her four sons. Her third son, Henry now became King Henry III. He was 22 years old. Catherine was determined that he would be a strong King. Henry was determined to be his own master. Though he kept many of Catherine's advisors as his own, he wanted to rule in his own name.

During the first ten years of Henry's reign there were three outbreaks of civil war between Protestant and Catholic. By most historians, these are called the Fifth War (1575-76), the Sixth War (1576-1577), and the Seventh War (1579-1580) in the French "Wars of Religion." Each of them involved fighting between the three factions in France: The French Protestants (known as the Huguenots), the Catholic League (an alliance of French nobles led by Henry, Duke of Guise), and the forces loyal to King Henry III. The Huguenots were supported by Protestant England and some of the Protestant princes in Germany. The Catholic League was supported by King Philip II of Spain and by the Pope. The French King was often in command of fewer resources, and fewer soldiers than either of the two rival parties.

Catherine did all she could to support her son, King Henry III. He married a princess from Lorraine, (named Louise), a year after becoming King. Unless he had a son, however, the next person in the line of succession would be Henry's younger brother, Catherine's fourth and youngest son, Hercule François, Duke of Anjou and Alençon, usually called Alençon.

In 1579, when Alençon was 24, Catherine made inquiries as to whether Queen Elizabeth of England would consider him as a suitor for her hand in marriage. The response from Queen Elizabeth was encouraging and the young man departed for England to court the 46-year-old virgin Queen. Elizabeth and Alençon quickly became friends and she seemed to be seriously considering giving her consent to marry him. But Elizabeth's advisors were very much opposed. They objected to Alençon's religion (Catholic), his nationality (French), and his mother (Catherine de' Medici) – whom most Englishmen believed was a terribly wicked woman, personally responsible for the St.

Hercule Francois,
Duke of Alencon

Bartholomew's Day Massacre. After two years in which Elizabeth expressed her affection to

Alençon, but her reservations about marrying him, Alençon finally gave up and left. He was the only foreign suitor who had ever come to court her in person.

Alençon left for the Netherlands, where William the Silent had invited him to become the hereditary ruler of the United Provinces. The Spanish King Philip had inherited the territory from his father, Charles V, but had been unsuccessfully attempting to put down revolt and heresy for ten years. Alençon's first action was to attempt to occupy Antwerp, the largest city of the seventeen provinces. It had been sacked by Spanish troops in 1576, but they had been withdrawn. However, the citizens of Antwerp were just as opposed to French troops as they were to Spanish.

On January 17 1583, Alençon asked to be permitted to enter the city and to honor them with a parade. As soon as the troops entered the city, the gates were slammed shut behind them. The French troops were trapped and began to be bombarded from windows and rooftops with stones, rocks, logs and even heavy chains. The city's garrison then opened a deadly, point-blank fire. Only a few Frenchmen, including the Alençon, escaped. Over 1500 troops perished, many of them hacked to death by the enraged citizens of Antwerp.

Alençon now fell ill with malaria. He was brought back to Paris, where his mother despaired over the prospect of burying another of her sons. In spite of her efforts to nurse him back to health, he died in February of 1584.

The situation in France now became grave for Catherine and her only surviving son, King Henry III. Henry and his wife had been married for nine years, but had no children. With the death of Alençon, the new heir to the throne was a distant cousin of Catherine's dead husband Henry II, none other than Henry of Navarre, the leader of the French Huguenots.

Henry, Duke of Guise was furious at the prospect of a protestant king of France. He was determined that such a catastrophe could not be permitted to happen. He sought the support of the King of Spain, Philip II, who signed a secret treaty with Duke Henry, promising to support him with money and troops to fight against the heretic Protestants.

Henry of Valois, King Henry III of France	Henry, Duke of Guise Head of the Catholic League	Henry of Navarre, Leader of the Huguenot party

Thus began the war of the three Henrys: **Henry of Valois**, King of France; **Henry Duke of Guise**, leader of the Catholic League; and **Henry of Navarre**, leader of the Huguenots. This was the eighth and final war in the French wars of religion.

When King Henry III recognized Henry of Navarre as his heir, Duke Henry of Guise resolved to overthrow the King. In the summer of 1588, with the support of the Spanish, Duke Henry organized a popular uprising in Paris. The King issued orders forbidding Duke Henry from entering the city, but the Duke defied the King. King Henry, with his troops outnumbered, sent for his mother, Catherine and implored her to intervene and persuade Duke Henry to withdraw his troops. Catherine's appeal was rejected by the Duke. King Henry was forced to sign a humiliating agreement in which he promised never to conclude a truce or peace with the "heretics", to forbid public office to any who would not take a public oath that they were a Catholic and never to leave the throne to a prince who was not Catholic.

King Henry was humiliated, but he swore he would have his revenge. Five months later, when Duke Henry paid a visit to the King at his castle of Blois, the King summoned him, alone, to a private visit. When the Duke entered the King's rooms, nine of his guards leapt from behind the curtains and killed the Duke. The next day, they killed his brother, the Cardinal of Guise.

King Henry went to see his mother and proudly announced what he had done. "At last, I am truly King of France again." Catherine is said to have replied, "God grant that you do not become king of nothing at all."

One month later, Catherine died, at the age of sixty-nine. Born in Florence, brought up in Rome, a princess at the court in Paris, she had been Queen at twenty-eight, and then widowed at forty. She had buried three of her four sons and two of her three daughters. Three of her sons had been crowned kings of France. Her eldest daughter, Elizabeth had married the King of Spain, but died when she was twenty-three. Her second daughter, Claude had married the Duke of Lorraine, but had died in 1575 at the age of twenty-eight. Only her son Henry III and her daughter Marguerite, married to Henry of Navarre, survived her.

Catherine's life can only be described as tragic. She was a woman of great ability and had great ambitions for her husband and her children. But on more than one occasion she chose to order the murder of her enemies. Her reputation will forever be stained with the responsibility for the St. Bartholomew's Day Massacre. At her death, all that she had worked for seemed to be slipping away.

INTRO!!!
(sent. 1)

Henry of Navarre

Born in 1553, King Henry IV of France from 1589 - 1610

In the year 1569 the Catholics of France and the Huguenots had been engaged in a bitter and bloody war for seven years. Although religion played a great part in the war it was just as much about the rivalries between the great nobles of France.

In the early summer of that year the Catholics won a great victory near the town of Jarnac. Among those who fell in the battle was the great Protestant leader, Louis, Prince of Condé.

The remnant of the Protestant army lay in camp near the castle of Cognac. They were sad and dispirited. Suddenly trumpets and drums were heard in the distance. A sentry announced that a band of soldiers was approaching. It was soon learned that they were allies not enemies. The defeated Protestants were very glad to see them.

They proved to be the escort of Jeanne d'Albert, Queen of Bearn, a little kingdom in the extreme southwest of France. As soon as she had heard of the death of Condé she had hastened to the Protestant camp.

The army was drawn up to receive her. Stepping forward, and holding her son by the hand, she said, "My friends, our cause has not died with the Prince of Condé. We have still left us brave captains. I offer to you as leader, Condé's nephew, my son, the Prince of Navarre."

With loud shouts of "Long live Henry, the Prince of Navarre," the soldiers at once elected him as their commander-in-chief.

Prince Henry was the son of Anthony of Bourbon and Queen Jeanne. He was born in 1553, and therefore was but sixteen years old when called to fill this high position. He was too young to lead the troops in battle; but he was ready to learn how to do so. The brave Gaspard de' Coligny agreed to instruct him, and to command the Protestant forces until he was able to do so.

Henry was a sturdy and well-grown lad. His life had been a simple one. His principal food had been the brown bread, the chestnuts, and such other plain fare as was eaten by the peasant boys who lived among the mountains of his mother's kingdom. He would have been glad to go out to battle at once; but the wise Coligny would not permit him.

Henry was very fond of reading. His favorite books were those containing the stories of the great conquerors of former times. He also read, many times over, the story of the good knight Bayard—the knight without fear and without reproach—who had lived not very long before.

When not yet twenty years old, Henry was married to Marguerite of Valois, sister of the king of France. The king's family, especially his mother Catherine de' Medici, hoped that this marriage would bring peace to the country. Many of the Huguenot leaders, and their families had come to Paris to attend the wedding. But a few days after the wedding, shortly after midnight, in the early morning hours of August 24, the great bell on the Palace of Justice awakened the people of Paris. This was a signal, and the soldiers of the Catholic party now began to attack the Huguenots. They were forced from the inns and mansions where they had been staying and murdered in the streets. When news of this massacre reached other French cities similar attacks were made and a great many Protestants were slain. The number has been variously estimated, some authorities stating that several thousand in all were killed, others that the number reached a hundred thousand. This was called the massacre of St. Bartholomew, because it happened on St. Bartholomew's Day.

The young Prince Henry was spared, but many of his friends were killed. He was afterwards kept a prisoner in the king's palace for nearly four years. Then he escaped and again became the leader of the Huguenots.

He was so anxious for the restoration of peace that he sent to Henry, the Duke of Guise, who commanded the Catholic army, this challenge: "I offer to end the quarrel. Either I will fight with you alone, or two on our side will fight with two on yours, or ten with ten, or whatever number you please; so as to stop the shedding of blood and the misery of the poor." But the duke would not accept the challenge, and the war went on.

Henry III, King of France, was a very weak and foolish man. So the Duke of Guise determined to dethrone him and make himself king. After the Duke seized control of Paris and many other parts of the country, King Henry summoned the Duke to his chambers where members of his bodyguard murdered the duke. Afterwards, the king said to his mother, who was very ill: "How do you feel?" "Better," she answered. "So do I," said the king. "This morning I have become king of France again. The king of Paris is dead."

The friends of the murdered duke at once took up arms against King Henry; and the Sorbonne—the great religious authority in Paris—declared that the people were no longer bound to obey him. Then King Henry III turned for help to his cousin, Henry of Navarre. They agreed to fight side by side against those who had revolted; and many of the Catholics joined with the Huguenots in order to bring about peace.

The Catholic rebels attacked King Henry near the city of Tours; but the Prince of Navarre marched to his aid, and the rebels left the field in great haste. As the Catholic rebels had failed to conquer the French king in battle, they determined to have him murdered. They found a man to carry out their plot. One morning, he gained admission to the king's presence by saying that he desired to see him on important business. As soon as they were left alone, the murderer handed Henry a letter. While the king was reading it, he drew a knife from his sleeve and plunged it into his body.

A messenger was sent in haste to tell Henry of Navarre. As he entered the king's room the tears gushed from his eyes, and he kissed the dying man with great tenderness. Many of the nobility of France had, by this time, come in to see their dying ruler. King Henry begged them to acknowledge Henry of Navarre as his lawful successor. All present agreed to do so. So the Prince of Navarre became king of France, with the title of Henry IV.

The Catholic rebels were not satisfied with this arrangement, since the law of the kingdom declared that no man could be king unless he were a Catholic. They demanded that Cardinal de Bourbon, Henry's uncle, should be made king with the title of Charles X.

Preparations were made for a great battle near the town of Arques. During the night the forces of the new king had dug trenches and thrown up earthworks so as to give them a greater advantage over the enemy. Next morning a rebel sentry, who had been captured during the night, was brought before him. As they talked together the man said, "We are about to attack you with thirty thousand foot and ten thousand horse. Where are your forces?"

"Oh," said the king, "you do not see them all. You do not count the good God and the good right; but they are ever with me."

A bloody battle followed, in which the king gained a wonderful victory. Soon after this he was joined by a body of English and Scotch soldiers sent him by Queen Elizabeth of England. His army was thus increased to over ten thousand men.

Then followed the famous battle of Ivry, in which the cannon, the colors, and nearly all the supplies of the Catholic rebels fell into the king's hands. On the rebel side the loss in killed, wounded and captured was over eleven thousand, while the king lost but five hundred men.

Henry IV at Ivry

Very soon after the battle of Ivry, Cardinal de Bourbon died. At about the same time the king laid siege to Paris which was still in the hands of the enemy.

Before closing up all the avenues of approach to Paris he wrote a letter to the governor of the city, in which he said: "I am anxious for peace. I love my city of Paris. She is my eldest daughter, and I wish to do her more favors than she asks." But it was all in vain, and the siege went on.

King Henry's army prevented the carrying of food into the city, and the people soon began to suffer. Bread gave out and the people were glad to eat rats, cats, dogs, horses, or anything else they could find to prevent starvation.

King Henry could not bear to hear of the suffering in Paris. He relaxed the siege and allowed the women and children to leave the city. He even permitted supplies to pass through his lines to relieve the besieged, saying, as he did so, "I do not wish to be king of the dead."

But just as Paris was on the point of surrendering, the Duke of Parma, one of the ablest generals in the service of King Philip II of Spain, arrived with a large Spanish army and compelled Henry to raise the siege.

The king now felt that the only way in which he could give peace to his people was by uniting himself with the Catholic Church. At eight o'clock on the morning of July 23, 1593, robed in white satin, he marched with a bodyguard of soldiers to the church of St. Denis, near Paris. At the door of the church he was met by a cardinal, an archbishop, nine bishops and large numbers of clergy and monks.

"Who are you?" asked the archbishop.

"The king," replied Henry.

"What do you wish?" was the archbishop's next inquiry.

To this the king replied, "To be received into the Catholic Church." Then the king knelt and declared his belief, after which the archbishop forgave and then formally received him.

After this ceremony Henry was anointed at Chartres, and thus declared sovereign of the whole kingdom. Henry's great desire now was to make his people prosperous. He once said "I wish every peasant in France to have a fowl in the pot every Sunday."

To end all further wars about religion, he signed and published the famous Edict of Nantes, in 1598. This royal decree gave the Protestants equal rights with the Catholics. The government agreed to pay the salaries of their clergy as well as those of the Catholics. Protestant children were allowed to enter the universities and colleges; their sick were received into the hospitals. The two great religious parties of the nation were placed upon a common footing.

The last years of King Henry IV were years of peace and prosperity. The farmers and trades-people were happy. The heavy debt which had lain for so many years upon France was entirely removed. The taxes were reduced to a rate lower than ever before.

In the midst of this growing sense of security and comfort all France was suddenly shocked and distressed beyond measure. A madman, by the name of Ravaillac, stabbed the king to the heart; and the career of the noble and generous Henry of Navarre was at an end.

The murder of King Henry IV of France

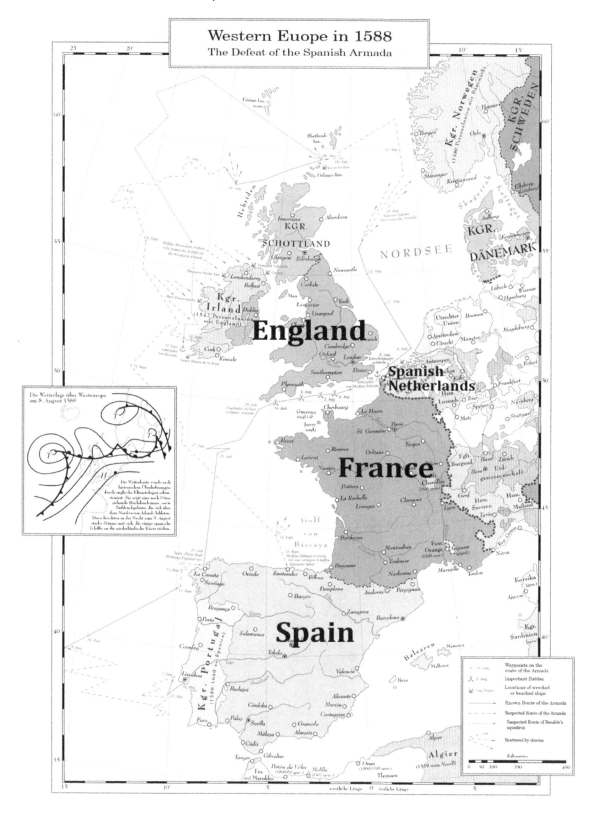

Western Euope in 1588
The Defeat of the Spanish Armada

Queen Elizabeth I
Born in 1533, Queen from 1558-1603

Queen Elizabeth I is one of the most admired of all the rulers of England. During her long reign she avoided the religious civil wars which were raging in France and brewing in Germany. She skillfully navigated the contentious rivalries of the French, the Germans, the Spanish, and the Dutch and (with one or two exceptions) kept England from becoming involved in a war with any of them. The one serious military threat of her rule – the attempted invasion by Spain in 1588 - ended with the miraculous scattering of the great Spanish fleet (the Armada) by her own small ships and nimble sailors and then by the providence of storms at sea.

During her reign, literature and the arts flourished in England. Scholars call it the Elizabethan Renaissance. During her last years, London and the court were dazzled by the plays of William Shakespeare. She had three or four serious suitors – among them two English noblemen and a French prince. But in the end, she would not consent to marry any of them. She left no heir to the throne. And yet remarkably, the succession in 1603 from Elizabeth to her cousin James, the King of Scotland was peaceful.

We know now that she ruled for 45 years. No one in her youth could have foreseen it. She was born in 1533. Her father was King Henry VIII. Her mother was Queen Anne Boleyn, Henry's second wife. At the time of her birth, she became the heir to the throne. Her older half-sister Mary had been removed from the line of succession when Henry had his first marriage annulled. Elizabeth's mother, Anne Boleyn, was pregnant again in 1534 and in 1536, but had miscarriages both times. When Elizabeth was two-and-a-half, Henry became convinced that

Queen Anne Boleyn had betrayed him. Anne was tried, convicted, and executed in May of 1536. Elizabeth was declared to be illegitimate and deprived of the title of princess. But her father did not send her away from court. Instead, she was brought up at the palace alongside her younger half-brother Edward, born when she was four. She was given an excellent education. By the time she was eleven, she could read and write English, Latin, and Italian. By the time she was seventeen, she was also fluent in French and Greek. In many ways, she was the best educated woman of her generation.

But though her father was King Henry VIII, it now seemed unlikely that she would ever be Queen. Henry VIII had three living children at the time he died in 1547. In his will he specified that he should succeeded by his son Edward, then nine years old, followed by his oldest daughter Mary (then 31) , if Edward should have no heir. And if Edward and Mary should both die without heirs, then and only then would his youngest daughter, Elizabeth (age 14) become Queen.

Edward VI, King of England

Edward ruled for six years, and then died in 1553, three months before what would have been his sixteenth birthday. Edward had followed the lead of the nobles who dominated the Regency Council; first Edward Seymour, Duke of Somerset and then John Dudley, Duke of Northumberland. On religious matters, he was advised by Thomas Cranmer, Archbishop of Canterbury, and authorized the continuation of the Protestant Reformation of the Church of England begun by his father.

When Edward died, his older half-sister Mary became Queen. She had both the Duke of Northumberland and Archbishop Cranmer executed for treason and heresy. She restored the relationship between the Church of England and the Roman Catholic Church. Those who stubbornly persisted in holding protestant views were persecuted and often executed, including four protestant bishops: Hooper, Latimer, Ridley, and Cranmer.

Shortly after becoming Queen, Mary accepted a marriage proposal from Prince Philip of Spain, the son of the German Emperor Charles V. They were married in July of 1554. Philip stayed in England for only about a year and then left for Spain. Though he returned for a brief visit in 1557, they had no children. The marriage was very unpopular in England. Many of the nobles grumbled that Mary should have married an Englishman. When plans for the marriage were announced, there was a brief rebellion in Kent. Mary's advisors suspected Elizabeth of having conspired with the rebels, and she was arrested and imprisoned in the Tower of London for two months. Then

Mary Tudor,
Queen of England

she was moved to a residence in Woodstock, near Oxford, where she was kept under house arrest for nearly a year.

In April of 1555, Mary announced she was pregnant. Elizabeth was recalled to court. If Mary and her child died, Elizabeth would become queen. If, on the other hand, Mary gave birth to a healthy child, Elizabeth's chances of becoming queen would become remote. But Mary was not pregnant. It now became clear to everyone that she was unlikely to have any children at all. Although Mary was not old, (she was just 39) she was not in good health. More and more, everyone in England now began to believe that Elizabeth would soon be Queen.

By the summer of 1558, it was known that Mary's health was failing. In November, she officially designated Elizabeth as her heir. Eleven days later she died. Two members of the Privy Council traveled to Elizabeth's residence in Hatfield to tell her the news. When they knelt in her presence and proclaimed her Queen Elizabeth, she was speechless. Then she knelt in prayer herself and quoted Psalm 118, verse 23: "This was the Lord's doing, and it is marvelous in our eyes."

Queen Elizabeth was 25 when she became queen. She had grown up at the court of Henry VIII. She had seen the intrigues which swirled through the palace during the brief reign of her younger brother Edward. Though she had kept her own counsel, she had been imprisoned

Queen Elizabeth I
Coronation Portrait

and suspected of treason by her older sister, Mary. Now she was Queen. Her first task was to settle the strife over religion which threatened the peace of her kingdom. Then she must seek to defend England, small and relatively weak, from the ambitions of the King of Spain, the King of France, and the German Emperor. And she must deal with the question of who would be her heir and successor. Unlike Edward and Mary, she had no other siblings who were obvious heirs.

To settle the question of religion, Elizabeth and her advisors submitted bills to Parliament which reaffirmed the independence of the English church from the Bishop of Rome, and named the Queen as the "Supreme Governor" of the English church – a slight alteration from the title claimed by her father as "Supreme Head" of the English church. The bills also revived and re-enacted the reforms of the English church which had been made by the martyred Archbishop Cranmer and by her younger brother Edward. Cranmer's Prayer Book became the official and only authorized liturgy of the English church once again.

The religious reforms were greeted with relief by many. Those of the clergy who remained loyal to the Roman Catholic Church resigned their positions or were removed. But none were executed. Those who thought that Elizabeth's reforms did not go far enough were at least relieved that the persecution of Protestants and the revival of the Catholic Church in England had been brought to an end. Many of the leading Protestants who had gone into exile, to Lutheran German cities or to Calvinist Geneva, returned and hoped for a more far-reaching reformation of the church in England. In particular, many of them wanted to do away with bishops and implement congregational appointment of ministers. They continued to oppose many of the forms of the Roman Catholic worship service which Elizabeth's reforms left unchanged. In time, those who wanted a more thorough-going reformation, who wanted to complete the purification of the English church, came to be known as Puritans. But for now, they were a small minority. Elizabeth's reforms were favored overwhelmingly.

Elizabeth was cautious in her dealings with the other great powers of Europe. She turned down an offer of marriage from her former brother-in-law, the King of Spain – though she did so politely. She quietly offered her support (in the form of money and supplies) to the Protestants in the Netherlands (who were fighting for independence from Catholic Spain) and to the Protestants in France (who were fighting for their existence). Although she briefly sent a small force to the French channel port of Le Havre to assist the French Huguenots, she was much chastened when her small force was defeated and forced to evacuate. She remained ever after very cautious about sending English troops on any foreign expeditions.

In 1567, the Protestant nobles in Scotland overthrew their catholic queen, Mary and she fled to England, where she asked for (and received) a safe haven from Elizabeth. Although Elizabeth protected her from her Scottish enemies, she would not allow Mary to use England as a base to regain her throne.

During the 1560's as Elizabeth celebrated her 27th, then 28th, then 29th, and then her 30th birthday, her advisors (and even occasionally, Parliament – much to her annoyance) continued to urge her to decide on a husband, so that she could marry and have children and be able to designate a young prince as heir to the throne. She continued to rebuff them. She was very close to one of her oldest friends, Robert Dudley, the Earl of Leicester and may have had romantic feelings for him. They were almost exactly the same age and had known each other since childhood. But when she was crowned Queen he was already married. It did not help matters any when

Robert Dudley
Earle of Leicester

Dudley's wife was found dead, with a broken neck, at the foot of a shallow flight of stairs in

1560. Although she briefly considered marrying Dudley, Elizabeth seems to have realized that such a marriage would have provoked outrage and controversy. Nevertheless, they remained close. The only breach in their friendship came in 1573, when he re-married without giving Elizabeth any advance notice. Elizabeth banished him from court and it was years before she allowed him to return.

In 1585, Elizabeth appointed Dudley to command an English army she was dispatching to aid the Dutch Protestants in their protracted attempt to win independence from Spain. He and his small force proved unable to do much of assistance, and were defeated in their one battle with Spanish forces. He returned to England, and during the summer of 1588 as England anxiously prepared for the invasion forces carried by the Spanish armada, Elizabeth placed him in overall command of the troops along the coast of the English Channel. The armada was defeated in the channel and the Spanish troops never landed. Dudley died a month later. He was 55. Elizabeth was distraught when she was told that her friend had died. She had recently received a letter that he had sent her only days before his death, and she now wrote on it "His Last letter." She put it in her treasure box, and it was still there when she died 15 years later.

Hercule Francois,
the Duke of Alençon

After she had decided against marrying Dudley in the late 1560's, Elizabeth kept her own counsel about who she would marry and discouraged those around her from even bringing the subject up. And then, in 1579 she received a message from Catherine de' Medici, the Queen mother in France. Catherine had been widowed in 1559, the same year that Elizabeth had been crowned. Two of her sons had become Kings of France and died after ruling for only a few short years. Her third son, Henry had been King of France for five years now. Her fourth son, Hercules Francois, the Duke of Alençon was 24 and she was seeking to arrange a marriage for him. Elizabeth was flattered, and though she was now 46, she took the suggestion seriously. The Duke of Alençon was invited to visit England so that he and Queen

Elizabeth might become better acquainted. He was the only one of her many foreign suitors who came to court her in person. She seems to have taken a liking to him, and did not discourage his suit. But as his visit stretched on, her advisors became more and more vocal in their opposition to the proposed match. He was Catholic. He was French. His mother was Catherine de' Medici, who had plotted the St. Bartholomew's Day Massacre of French Protestants! At last, Elizabeth was forced to concede that the proposed marriage would be unwise. But she did like her "little frog," as she playfully called him. He, in turn, gave her a frog-shaped earring which she often wore. When he left England in 1581, she wrote a poem, entitled **"On Monsieur's Departure,"**

> I grieve and dare not show my discontent,
> I love and yet am forced to seem to hate,
> I do, yet dare not say I ever meant,
> I seem stark mute but inwardly do prate.
> I am and not, I freeze and yet am burned,
> Since from myself another self I turned.
>
> My care is like my shadow in the sun,
> Follows me flying, flies when I pursue it,
> Stands and lies by me, doth what I have done.
> His too familiar care doth make me rue it.
> No means I find to rid him from my breast,
> Till by the end of things it be supprest.
>
> Some gentler passion slide into my mind,
> For I am soft and made of melting snow;
> Or be more cruel, love, and so be kind.
> Let me or float or sink, be high or low.
> Or let me live with some more sweet content,
> Or die and so forget what love ere meant.

The Duke of Alençon departed England for the Netherlands. There he took command of French troops on an expedition to help the Dutch Protestants in their rebellion from Spain. He did this not from any personal religious sympathy for the Protestant faith, but because Spain was the great rival and enemy of France. His expedition, as you have already read, ended in failure and he died shortly thereafter. At about the same time, the Dutch nobleman who had led the revolt for seventeen years, William of Orange, was assassinated. The Spanish general in the

Netherlands, the Duke of Parma moved rapidly and occupied a number of key Dutch cities. The Dutch sent ambassadors to England begging Elizabeth to send help. Her advisors thought she should give it. If the Dutch were defeated, then the threat of a Spanish invasion of England would be large. As a result, Elizabeth sent a small military force under the command of one of her former suitors, Robert Dudley. The active intervention of the English in the Dutch rebellion, in turn, provoked Philip II to launch an invasion to conquer England with Spanish troops – for he had become convinced that his armies would never defeat the Dutch Protestants so long as the English continued to support them. Philip was also annoyed by the repeated attacks by English privateers on Spanish ships and possessions in the new world and against the annual Atlantic treasure fleets.

Mary, Queen of Scots

Relations between England and Spain had also been soured by the discovery of a plot by a group of English Catholic noblemen to assassinate Elizabeth, free Mary of Scotland from her "house arrest" in northern England and proclaim her the true Queen. The plotters wrote letters to Mary in which they assured her that King Philip of Spain had promised to send troops to support the plot. Fifteen noblemen were tried and executed. Mary of Scotland was also tried, found guilty and condemned to death. Elizabeth hesitated before giving her consent to Mary's execution, but in the end she did so and Mary was beheaded in February of 1587.

Thus, the stage was set for the great Spanish Armada and the Spanish attempt to conquer England of 1588. Philip assembled a fleet of 130 ships, 8,000 sailors, and 18,000 soldiers. The plan was for this fleet to rendezvous with an additional 30,000 soldiers under the command of the Duke of Parma in the Netherlands and ferry them across the channel for a quick and overwhelming march on London.

The English ships were smaller than the Spanish galleons, but there were more of them – and they were faster. They repeatedly sailed in close to the Spanish galleons, fired their guns, and then darted away before the Spanish could close on them and board them. After five days of fighting in the channel, the Spanish were tired and frustrated. They attempted to regroup off the port of Calais, but during the night the English took their oldest ships, set them on fire and released them where the wind would carry them into the anchored ships of the Armada. Many of the Spanish captains panicked and cut their anchor cables, sailing away from the fireships as quickly as they could. The next day the English resumed their attacks and the Armada was slowly forced into the North Sea and up the coast of England – away

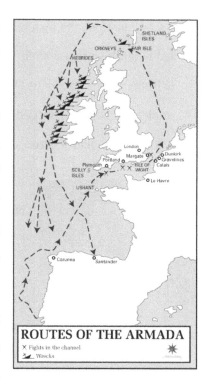

from the Dutch coast where the Duke of Parma's army waited. The Spanish abandoned their invasion plans and attempted to sail around the northern coasts of Scotland and Ireland and return to Spain. Half the ships were wrecked by storms and the treacherous rocks and reefs along the coast. In the end, only 54 of the 130 ships made it back to Spain.

Both Elizabeth and the English took the defeat of the Armada as a symbol of God's favor and an elaborate thanksgiving service was conducted at St. Paul's Cathedral in London. There were also commemorative medals struck, including one playful one with the inscription "veni, vidi, fugit" (he came, he saw, he fled).

Elizabeth continued to reign for fifteen more years after the defeat of the Spanish Armada. The victory had stirred the population in England. They were now more fervently patriotic and Protestant – and they loved their Queen. It was in the last years of her reign that William Shakespeare appeared on the scene and began his twenty year career, writing a series of plays that charmed and dazzled audiences and celebrated the history and virtues of England.

In 1594, the Irish rebelled against English rule and English settlements. The rebellion was led by an Irish clan leader, Hugh O'Neill, the Earl of Tyrone. He was joined by the leader of the O'Donnell clan, known as "Red Hugh." At first, the rebellion did not seem serious to the English noblemen who had settled in Ireland, but the rebels gathered strength and support and their army grew rapidly in size.

Robert Devereaux
the Earl of Essex

After the Irish rebels had defeated the English in several battles, Elizabeth sent her court favorite, Robert Devereux, Earl of Essex in command of an army of 17,000 men to put an end to the rebellion. Essex did not prove to be much of a military commander. He suffered a series of embarrassing defeats and eventually negotiated a truce with Hugh O'Neill and the Irish rebels, without seeking the Queen's leave to do so. Then, to defend his actions, he left his post in Ireland and returned to London to seek an audience with the Queen. Although the Queen had expressly forbidden him to return, he presented himself in her bedchamber one morning at Nonsuch Palace and begged her forgiveness and favor. Although Elizabeth liked him, she was much annoyed at his behavior. She dismissed him and ordered him placed under house arrest until the Privy Council could decide what to do.

The Privy Council took six months to decide. Finally, in June of 1600, Essex was tried before a special commission and removed from all his offices. Essex was embarrassed and humiliated. Without his position at court and the offices to which Elizabeth had appointed him, he was also broke. Eight months later, in February of 1601, he left his house in London with a group of armed followers and marched towards the palace. What he intended has never been entirely clear – he may not have been sure himself what he wanted. He seems to have believed that the people of London would join him in his march on the palace and that his popularity would force Elizabeth to re-admit him to court. There is some evidence that he hoped to seize her and proclaim himself her "protector" and rule England himself in her name.

But no one in London joined him, and Elizabeth was outraged. Essex was tried on a charge of treason, found guilty, and executed within three weeks. He was the last person beheaded in the Tower of London. Elizabeth is said to have wept for days.

Within a year of Essex's death, it was clear that Elizabeth was not well. Six months after his death, she celebrated her 68th birthday. She still refused to name an heir and successor, but her advisors began a discreet correspondence with her cousin, the King of Scotland, James VI (later James I of England). Although she would not formally name him as her heir, she let it be known that she was content that he should succeed her.

After her 69th birthday in the fall of 1602 she fell sick and spent much time alone in her apartments, though she long resisted getting into bed. After several months of illness, she died during the night of March 23/24 at Richmond Palace. She had been Queen for forty-five years.

In her final speech to Parliament, in 1601, she had remarked wearily that "To be a King, and wear a Crown, is a thing more glorious to them that see it, than it is pleasant to them that bear it".

Although her people had loved her, England was ready for a change. But what sort of King would James of Scotland be?

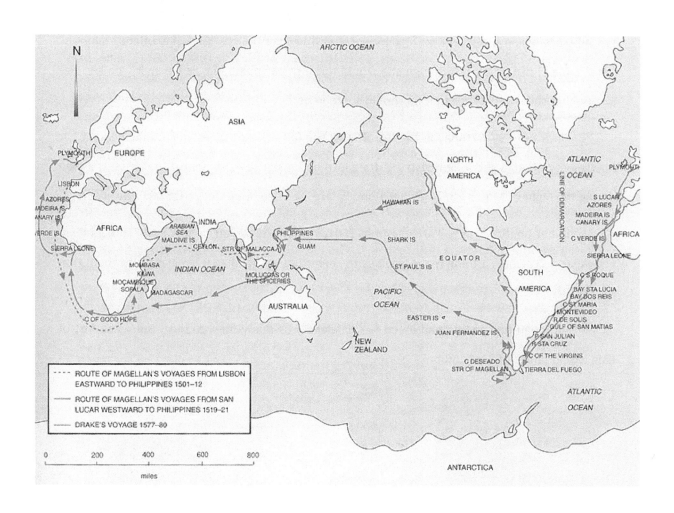

Sir Francis Drake

1540–1596

It was during Elizabeth's reign that England first became a great naval power. Among the men who helped to make her so, none were more famous than Sir Francis Drake. There is some doubt about the date of Drake's birth. It is now generally believed that he was born in 1540, though some writers put the date at least five years earlier.

Maybe born in 1540

Maybe?

The place of his birth was the little town of Tavistock, in Devonshire. He had a great love for the sea even when but a child. His parents were too poor to help him into a good position, and so he began his career at sea as a cabin boy. But he had the merit of pluck; and he soon rose to the highest rank in the English navy.

In 1567 he went with his uncle Sir John Hawkins, who was one of the noted sailors of that day, on a slave-trading voyage to Africa and the West Indies. The experiences he met with at that time gave color to the rest of his life.

Being driven out of their course by storms, they were obliged to seek shelter in the harbor of San Juan de Ulua, a Spanish port on the coast of Mexico. There they were received with a show of kindness, but were afterwards attacked by a superior force, and only two vessels escaped. After this act of treachery, Drake resolved to seize every opportunity to plunder the Spaniards and thus to make good the loss which he and his uncle had sustained.

In the years 1570–71 Drake made two voyages to the West Indies for the purpose of becoming acquainted with the situation and strength of the Spanish settlements. In 1572, he sailed again with two ships from England to the Caribbean. His plan was to capture the town of

Wanted to capture Nombre de Dios

Nombre de Dios on the Isthmus of Panama, which was the port the Spaniards used to ship to Spain the gold and silver taken from the mines of Peru.

In the attempt to take this town Drake was severely wounded. He tried to conceal his hurt from his men as they pressed onward into the town. But just as they reached the market place where they hoped to find the treasure, he fainted from loss of blood. His men at once carried him to his ship, and the enterprise was abandoned.

As soon as he was able to do so, he began to sail back and forth along the coast. He seized a large number of ships, and took from them a great amount of wealth both in money and goods. He formed an alliance with a band of run-away slaves called Cimarrones and together they built a fort on a small island at the mouth of a river. There Drake and his men remained until February 3, 1573.

On that day Drake set out, with some Cimarrones as guides, to cross the Isthmus of Panama and gain his first view of the Pacific Ocean. Half way across the isthmus they led him to a tall tree standing on a central hill. Among the topmost branches of this tree there was a platform on which ten or twelve men might stand at ease. Drake climbed up to this platform, and was delighted to find that from his lofty perch he could see both the Atlantic and the Pacific.

Drake returned to England in the fall of 1573, carrying much treasure which he divided with the strictest fairness among his followers. His own share was large enough to enable him to purchase three ships. With these he sailed to Ireland, and there, as a volunteer under the Earl of Essex, he "did most excellent service."

But Francis Drake is chiefly distinguished as the first Englishman who sailed round the world. In December, 1577, with five little vessels, about the size of those of Columbus, he sailed out of the harbor of Plymouth. It took him seven months to reach Patagonia (the southern part of South America), and there he remained for about nine weeks. Two of his ships had become so leaky as to be unfit for further service, and he was compelled to abandon them. The crews and stores were taken on board the other vessels and the fleet started out to sail through Magellan

Strait in order to reach the Pacific. It had been sixty years since Magellan had passed through the strait, but Drake's was the first English expedition to follow the great Portuguese navigator over this route.

While the vessels were in the strait, one of those terrific storms arose for which the region of Cape Horn is still noted. One ship called the *Marigold* was never heard of again, and the crew of the *Elizabeth* were so disheartened by the terrible weather that they put about and returned to England. Although Drake was left with but a single ship he would not give up the voyage. He made his way into the Pacific, and sailed northward along the coasts of Chile and Peru.

The Spaniards had already established colonies on the western shores of South America. Santiago had been founded nearly forty years before, and Lima was already a town of considerable size. As Spain and England were not friendly toward each other, it was thought perfectly right to capture Spanish vessels and to plunder Spanish towns. Queen Elizabeth in fact had given Drake a commission, signed with her own hand, authorizing him to do this. ☀

Queen Elizabeth gave Drake special permission to plunder/capture Spanish towns

After plundering a number of the Spanish settlements he sailed north until he reached the western coast of North America. Finding that his ship was again in need of repairs, he landed for that purpose at a point which has since been named Drakes Bay, a little to the north of San Francisco Bay.

Drakes Bay

From California he sailed across the Pacific and visited the Spice Islands and Java. Leaving Java he crossed the Indian Ocean and passed around the Cape of Good Hope into the Atlantic. Then, steering northward, he made his way back to England, reaching home exactly two years and ten months after starting on the voyage.

On his arrival a banquet was prepared on board the ship in which he had sailed round the world. Queen Elizabeth was one of the guests. In honor of his achievement she knighted him on the deck of his ship, and it was in this way that he came to be called Sir Francis Drake.

① Francis Drake
↓
② knighted
↓
③ Sir Francis Drake

The little vessel had been so battered by the storms through which it had passed that it was unfit for further service. But Elizabeth gave orders that it should be carefully preserved as a monument to its famous captain. One hundred years later it was found that the timbers were badly decayed. It was then broken up. One piece of the wood, that was still sound, was made into a chair for King Charles II, who afterwards gave it to the University of Oxford, where it can still be seen.

one piece of wood still around

Drake's Expedition to Cadiz

A few years later, Sir Francis rendered another valuable service to his native land. England received intelligence that Philip of Spain was equipping an enormous fleet for the purpose of invading England. Drake learned that the larger part of this fleet was in the harbor of Cadiz, making final preparations for the voyage. He was then at Lisbon with thirty English war ships under his command. He at once sailed for Cadiz, and, on arriving, he sent a fire-ship among the Spanish vessels, burned nearly a hundred of them, and escaped from the harbor unharmed. This delayed the sailing of the Spanish fleet for nearly a year, and when at length it approached the shores of England, Drake did more, perhaps, than any other man to bring about its overthrow.

Spaniard's army = "Invincible Armada"

The Spaniards had collected about one hundred and thirty vessels of war, and more than fifty thousand men, and to this array they gave the proud title of the "Invincible Armada." Thirty-five thousand men were to land at the mouth of the River Thames and another large force was to land farther to the north. Then a third force threatened the west coast. In this way England was to be attacked at three different points at the same time. The Spaniards thought that the English would be bewildered, and would surrender.

But all this great armament was not prepared without some news of it getting to England, and preparations were made to repel the foe.

Troops were collected at Tilbury ready to attack the Spaniards in case they succeeded in landing. The queen on horseback reviewed them, and made a stirring speech. The merchants of London and other ports offered their ships to be used as ships of war; the rich brought their treasures; the poor volunteered in the army and navy. Thus the coast was well guarded and the number of vessels in the fleet was increased from thirty to one hundred and eighty.

These carried about sixteen thousand men—not half the number on board the enemy's fleet—but they were sturdy English fighters. Howard was Lord High Admiral, and with him were Drake, Frobisher, and Hawkins, the most famous English mariners of the time.

One evening, late in July, 1588, beacon lights blazed all along the coast of the English Channel telling the news that the Spanish fleet was coming. Next morning, arranged in a crescent, the Armada moved up the Channel. Its line was seven miles long.

The English fleet sailed out from Plymouth. Its vessels were light, while those of the Spaniards were heavy, but more than this, the English ships were finely managed, and their guns were skillfully aimed, while most of the shots of the Spaniards went over the heads of the English. The Spaniards tried to come to close quarters, but the English vessels were so steered that this could not be done. Day after day for a week the fighting continued.

The Spanish commander then led his fleet into the harbor of Calais on the French side of the Channel. He wished to get provisions and powder and shot. He also wished to get some small vessels—swift sailors—with which he might match the light ships of his adversaries.

The English fleet followed, but the French would not allow them to attack the Spaniards in the harbor. To force them out into the open sea, the English turned eight of their oldest and poorest vessels into fireships. Tar, rosin and pitch were placed upon them. The masts and rigging were covered with pitch. Their guns were loaded; and thus, all ablaze, they were sent at midnight drifting into the harbor with wind and tide. This fire fleet did its work. It did not

Spanish ships under fire

succeed in setting fire any Spanish ship but it so alarmed the Spaniards that they cut their anchors free and sailed from the harbor into the open sea, and there the English attacked them. Many of their ships were disabled, and four thousand of their men were killed in one day's fighting.

Next day the Spanish commanders held a council of war. The question to be decided was whether to try to sail home through Howard's fleet or go round Scotland and avoid his guns. The Spanish officers decided to attempt the voyage round Scotland. So the whole remaining Spanish fleet of perhaps one hundred and twenty vessels steered toward the north.

On the coast of Scotland, there are dangerous rocks, and when the shattered Armada neared the Orkney Islands, violent storms arose, which wrecked many of the ships. Thus nature finished what man had begun—the ruin of the most powerful fleet that ever had sailed from the shores of Europe. Only fifty-four vessels and about ten thousand men succeeded in returning to Spain. About eighty ships had been destroyed, and thousands of men had perished.

Ten years after the destruction of the Armada, Sir Francis Drake made one more voyage to the West Indies. He still cherished the plan of seizing the town of Porto Bello on the Isthmus of Panama, and thus securing the gold and silver brought there for shipment to Spain. He was, however, again doomed to disappointment. He was stricken with fever, and died on board of his ship, January 28, 1596.

His body was buried at sea. Lord Macaulay wrote these lines in reference to his burial:

"The waves became his winding sheet:
The waters were his tomb.
But for his fame—the mighty sea
Has not sufficient room."

SIR WALTER RALEIGH

1552–1618

Sir Walter Raleigh was a famous Englishman who lived in the days of Queen Elizabeth. He was a soldier and statesman, a poet and historian, but the most interesting fact about him is that he was the first Englishman who attempted to plant colonies in the region now known as the United States.

He was born in Devonshire, England, in 1552. At about the time that he was growing up, great sympathy was felt in England for the Huguenots, as the French Protestants were called, and Raleigh enlisted as a volunteer in the Huguenot army. He was in France at the time of the massacre of St. Bartholomew, in 1572, but we do not know how long he remained there.

In 1580 he went to Ireland as captain of a company of a hundred men, to aid in putting down a rebellion there.

Returning to England at the age of thirty, he became one of Queen Elizabeth's courtiers. He constantly sought to please her. A story is told that one day when Elizabeth was out walking at Greenwich, she came to a muddy place. Raleigh was in attendance upon her, and quickly took off his costly coat and spread it over the mud so that it formed a carpet for the queen to walk on. This

gallant act is said to have gained him high favor from Elizabeth. Whether the story is true or not it is certain that for some years he was the greatest favorite at the court.

In Queen Elizabeth's reign the English began to take great interest in the new country of North America. Raleigh and his half-brother, Sir Humphrey Gilbert, obtained from Queen Elizabeth permission to colonize any land in North America which was not already claimed by a Christian nation. Five ships were fitted out and sailed from England, in 1583, under the command of Gilbert. Raleigh was unable to go, but he bore a large part of the expense of the expedition. Hardly had the voyage begun when one of the ships, owing to sickness among the crew, was obliged to return to England. Gilbert, with the other ships, kept on his course across the Atlantic, and at last reached Newfoundland, where he went on shore and took possession of the island in the name of Queen Elizabeth.

Gilbert sailed along the coast searching for a suitable place to found his colony. Near Cape Breton Island, the largest vessel stuck in the mud, and was broken to pieces by the force of the waves; all but fourteen, out of nearly a hundred men on board, lost their lives. Gilbert thought that now it would be impossible to carry out the colonization plan, so with his three remaining ships he started back to England.

A terrible storm came on, but the vessels kept together for a time. When last seen, Gilbert was sitting in the stern of his ship, reading a book. He shouted to those on board the other ships, "We are as near to heaven by sea as by land." During the night his ship disappeared, and not one on board was saved, but the other vessels succeeded in reaching England.

Raleigh was not discouraged by this failure. In the following year he sent another expedition to America. In due time his vessels reached the coast of what is now known as North Carolina. Everybody was charmed with the beauty of the country. But after exploring the coast for some distance, and taking possession of the region in the name of Elizabeth, the expedition for some reason returned to England without making a settlement.

The description which the explorers gave of the country which they had visited interested Queen Elizabeth. As she was called the "Virgin Queen," Raleigh suggested that she should give her name "Virginia" to the newly discovered territory. She did this, and the state of Virginia, which formed part of the territory thus discovered, obtained its name in that way.

Raleigh soon organized a third expedition which sailed in 1585 with about a hundred colonists. Seven vessels carried them. The fleet was commanded by Sir Richard Grenville while the colonists were in charge of a noted soldier named Ralph Lane. After a long voyage they reached Roanoke Island, on the coast of North Carolina. Grenville returned to England with the fleet, while Lane was left on Roanoke Island to establish a settlement.

The colonists probably quarreled with the Indians. Their provisions failed, and they could get none from the red men. No ship from England came with supplies, and the colonists were thoroughly discouraged. The next year a fleet under command of Sir Francis Drake called there by chance, and all the colonists returned home.

One of them, named Thomas Hariot, in an account of the colony, spoke of a herb "called by the natives yppomoc," and told how it was smoked by them in pipes. This herb was tobacco. Hariot and his companions had learned to like it, and they carried quantity home with them.

This was the first Virginia tobacco imported into England. Some of it was given to Raleigh who smoked it in silver pipes. Queen Elizabeth also learned the art, and she made smoking fashionable among people of high rank in England.

In 1587 Raleigh sent a fourth expedition to Virginia. It consisted of three ships carrying one hundred and fifty colonists under Captain White.

After landing his passengers White

Raleigh's servant misunderstands smoking

returned to England for supplies. When he got back to America, three years later, he found that the colonists had disappeared, and it was never learned what became of them. Thus failed Raleigh's last attempt to colonize Virginia.

So confident was he that the new world would be colonized, that he wrote of Virginia, "I shall yet live to see it an English nation." And this he did, for he lived until 1618, and Jamestown had then been founded ten years.

In return for his services in quelling the Irish rebellion the queen gave him a large grant of land in Ireland. The most interesting fact about this Irish property is that Raleigh raised there the first potatoes grown in Europe.

You have read how Philip II of Spain attempted, in 1588, to invade England with his famous Armada, and how that great fleet was destroyed. There was in England a great hatred of the Spaniards and a great desire to injure them. At that time Spain claimed most of the new world so far as it had been explored, and her ships were all the time coming home laden with the products of her possessions, and particularly with silver from her mines.

Raleigh fitted out privateers to capture such vessels, and on one of his voyages the main cargo ship of the Spanish "treasure fleet" was captured. She was the most valuable prize which, up to that time, had ever been brought into an English port. The queen herself had an interest in the expedition and was greatly pleased with her share of the plunder.

Raleigh had still a great desire to plant colonies, and he now turned his attention to South America. He placed a vessel in command of a certain Captain Whiddon, and sent him, in 1594, to explore the region now known as Guiana.

Fabulous stories had been told of the amount of gold in this province. It was said that the king of the natives there, when he was going to make an offering to his gods, covered his body all over with gold dust, and from this the Spaniards called him "El Dorado," that is, "the gilded man."

In 1595 Raleigh himself set sail with five ships for the land of "the Gilded King." He entered the mouth of the Orinoco and sailed up the great river for a distance of about four hundred miles. But the river rose so high that navigation was imperiled; and Raleigh therefore returned to the coast and soon afterward sailed back to England.

War with Spain continued. In 1597, an English expedition under Howard and Essex was fitted out to attack Cadiz, a seaport on the Spanish coast. Raleigh was in one of the ships and rendered important service. The English destroyed or captured the ships of a large Spanish fleet in the harbor, and the city itself surrendered. This exploit was one of the most brilliant ever achieved by the English navy. After it, the Spaniards never regained their power upon the sea.

All through the reign of Elizabeth, Raleigh was highly esteemed by the queen and by the people. Up to the date of her death he was a Member of Parliament. But, in 1603, James I succeeded Elizabeth. Raleigh's enemies spread a rumor that he had plotted against the new King. James believed the rumors. He conceived a dislike for Raleigh, and stripped him of all his offices. Raleigh was arrested and brought to trial. One who was present wrote that when the trial began, he would have gone a hundred miles to see him hanged; but that before it closed, he would have gone two hundred to save his life. Although nothing was proved against him, Raleigh was condemned to death. Only when he stood on the scaffold was his sentence changed to imprisonment for life.

For thirteen years he was confined in the Tower of London; and there he wrote his great work "**The History of the World**." It is reported that the Prince of Wales often visited him in the Tower, and said, "No man but my father would keep such a bird in such a cage."

In 1616 Raleigh was released so that he might go on another expedition to the golden land of Guiana and capture Spanish merchant vessels. But disease broke out among his crews, and Raleigh himself was stricken down with fever before they reached the Orinoco. His son was killed in a fight with the Spaniards; and, in 1618, the poor father returned to England broken-hearted.

Shortly after his return to England he was arrested and condemned to die the very next morning under the sentence of death which had been passed upon him fifteen years before.

Even then his courage did not leave him. On the scaffold he asked to see the axe. "This gives me no fear," he said. "It is a sharp medicine to cure me of all diseases." To someone who told him to lay his head toward the north, he replied, "What matter how the head lies, so the heart be right?"

Though they did not succeed, Raleigh's attempts at colonization were the beginnings of the great movement which led to the establishment of the Thirteen Colonies; and those colonies formed the basis for the United States of America.

Raleigh says goodbye to his wife

James I

Born in 1566, King of England 1603-1625

James Charles Stuart was born on June 19, 1566 at Edinburgh Castle in Scotland. His mother was Mary, the Queen of Scotland. His father was Henry Stuart, Duke of Albany, commonly known as Lord Darnley. When James was eight months old, his father was murdered. His mother was the chief suspect. The marriage between Mary and Henry had not been going well. It was Mary's second marriage. Her first husband had been the French prince, Francis – the eldest son of the French King Henry II. Mary had been Queen of Scotland since she was a week old. Her father had died just a few days after her birth and she inherited the throne. But because she was an infant, Scotland was ruled by a regent, the Earl of Arran, and by her mother, acting in her name. In 1548, Mary's mother arranged for an alliance between Scotland and France. The French sent troops to aid the Scots in resisting raids by the English. The Scots agreed that their little Queen would marry the heir to the French crown. Mary was sent from Scotland to France when she was five years old, already betrothed to be married. Her mother, Mary of Guise, widow of King James V, stayed behind in Scotland to rule in her name. In 1558, shortly before her 16th birthday, she and Francis were married.

When her father-in-law, King Henry III, was killed in a terrible accident the next summer, Francis and Mary became the King and Queen of France. Seventeen months later, Francis died and the crown passed to his younger brother, Charles IX. One year later, in 1561, Mary returned to Scotland, where she was still queen. She was nineteen years old, had spent most of her life at the French court, and was a widow. She was five years younger than her cousin, Elizabeth, the Queen of England, and like her, had to deal with a country divided by the conflict between Protestants and Catholics. Although Mary, herself, remained a Roman Catholic, she understood that the majority of her Scottish subjects had become Protestants. She promised her Scottish subjects that she would not alter or interfere in the reformation of the Scottish church – now led by John Knox and heavily influenced by John Calvin of Geneva.

The Scottish nobles accepted Mary as their Queen, but they were uneasy about the question of succession. Mary and Francis had not had any children. Her advisors and the Scottish nobility urged her to marry again and have children in order to provide an heir to the throne. In 1565, she married Henry Stuart, Lord Darnley. He, like she, was a grand-child of Mary Tudor, the daughter of Henry VII and sister of Henry VIII. The marriage did not go well. Darnley was arrogant, hot-headed, and quite jealous of his 27-year-old bride. Shortly after Mary announced that she was pregnant, Darnley became angry over the close friendship between Mary and her Italian secretary, David Rizzio. In March of 1566, Darnley broke into her rooms at the castle with a gang of his friends and murdered Rizzio in front of Mary, who was six months pregnant with James.

Mary was outraged, and Darnley fled Edinburgh. After the birth of their son, James, Mary's attitude towards Darnley appeared to soften. She learned that he had taken refuge in Glasgow and was seriously ill. She sent messengers to him and persuaded him to return to Edinburgh – but because of his illness he did not return to Edinburgh Castle, instead staying at a house just outside the city walls. Mary visited him frequently over the course of the first few weeks of 1567. Then, during the night of 10 February, 1567 a violent explosion completely destroyed the house where Darnley had been staying. His bedchamber had been on the second floor, and apparently, barrels of gunpowder had been set off in the cellar. Darnley's body was found lying in the gardens outside the house.

Suspicion fell on James Hepburn, the Earl of Bothwell – four years older than Mary, who had become her closest advisor after the death of Rizzio. Darnley's family brought charges against Bothwell for the murder of Darnley. After a day-long trial before the Scottish Privy Council, Bothwell was acquitted. Twelve days later, while Mary was traveling from Linlithgow Palace to Edinburgh, Bothwell suddenly appeared with 800 men and took Mary into his custody. Within three weeks, Bothwell had secured a divorce from his wife (whom he had married the year before) and married Mary, his captive Queen. It had been less than 90 days since the explosion that killed Darnley.

All this was too much for the people of Scotland and the Scottish nobles. They raised an army and marched on Bothwell's estates. Bothwell fled Scotland and Mary was forced to abdicate her title as Queen and allow her infant son, James VI to be crowned as King of Scotland. Mary was held under house arrest at Loch Leven Castle. James VI, barely one year old, was taken back to Edinburgh where he would be raised by a regency council of Protestant Scottish nobles. When James was two, his mother escaped her imprisonment. She quickly raised a small army in an attempt to seize Edinburgh and James. But she was defeated, and had to flee to England where she was placed under house arrest, on the orders of Queen Elizabeth. James never saw his mother again. After nineteen years as a prisoner in England, Mary was caught in a conspiracy to escape, murder Elizabeth, and seize the English crown. She was tried and executed in 1587.

By that time, James was nineteen years old, and had been ruling Scotland in his own name for several years. His younger years had been turbulent as the Scottish nobles fought each other over who would hold the title of regent. Regent Moray was assassinated in 1570, regent Stewart was fatally wounded in a raid by Mary's supporters in 1571. Regent Erskine died a year later, most likely poisoned. Regent Morton lasted ten years, but was overthrown in 1581 when James, then 15, conspired with a French nobleman, Esmé Stewart, to assert himself as King. He charged Morton with complicity in the murder of his father, Lord Darnley, and had him executed. He created Esmé Stewart as the Duke of Lennox – the only Duke in all of Scotland. The

Protestant nobles of Scotland distrusted him because he was French, and because up until his appointment as Duke, he had been a Catholic. Two of the Scottish nobles took matters into their own hands. They invited the young King to visit them at Ruthven castle and then made him their prisoner. They forced James to banish the Duke of Lennox from Scotland. Lennox died a year later in France.

The next year, the 17-year-old James managed to secure his freedom. His captors either fled Scotland or were arrested and executed for their treason.

Now that James had come of age, he faced the familiar task of monarchs – a marriage to ensure the line of succession. In 1589, James and his advisors settled on a match that seemed to

Anne of Denmark

please everyone – Princess Anne of Denmark. She was eight years younger than James, but at 15 deemed old enough to be a bride. She was from a royal family. She was Protestant. Perhaps best of all, she was NOT from any of the Scots clans and the marriage would not immediately elevate or antagonize any of their fierce rivalries. The Scottish nobles were equally pleased that she was not French and that there would be no attempt to revive the "auld alliance." In August of 1589, Anne set sail for Scotland from Denmark along with an escort of Danish noblemen and a party of Scots noblemen who had crossed over in order to escort her to Edinburgh. But the attempt to sail from Denmark to Scotland met with difficulties. A storm separated the ships and the *Gideon*, carrying Anne, returned to coast of Norway for repairs. A few days later one of the other ships in the fleet reached Edinburgh and reported the alarming news that Anne's ship was missing in the north Atlantic. James called for national fasting and public prayers for the safety of his bride. He even wrote songs and poetry, comparing his situation to the plight of Hero and Leander. After several weeks, word finally reached him that Anne was safe in Norway, but that the sailors declined to attempt another crossing until the spring. James impulsively decided that he would cross the ocean to retrieve his bride!

Accompanied by an entourage of 300, James arrived in Norway, married his betrothed, and spent the winter making a grand tour of the castles and courts of Norway and Denmark.

The following spring, the happy young couple arrived in Edinburgh and were given a public celebration. The fifteen-year-old Anne rode into Edinburgh in a solid silver coach brought over from Denmark, with her 24-year-old husband James riding on horseback alongside. In 1594, Anne gave birth to their first child, Henry Frederick. In 1596 and 1598, they were blessed with two daughters, Elizabeth and Margaret. Tragically, Margaret died at 18 months. In 1600, Charles was born. And in 1602, he was joined by a younger brother, Robert who unfortunately, died at four months. Two more daughters, Mary and Sophia were born in 1605 and 1606, but both died in infancy.

In 1603, when James' cousin Elizabeth I of England died, James became the King of England. For two years, he had maintained a secret correspondence with Elizabeth's chief minister, Sir Robert Cecil. Although Elizabeth never publicly named him as her heir, Cecil had already drawn up a proclamation naming James as the new King before Elizabeth died. James immediately set out from Edinburgh for London. Along the way, large crowds gathered, anxious for a glimpse of their new King.

Although the first year of his reign as King of England started auspiciously enough, there were some disquieting developments. The happy news was the successful negotiation of an end to the state of war between Spain and England which had existed since the days of the Spanish Armada, nearly twenty years before. Sir Robert Cecil had been working quietly to achieve this result, and James was impressed and grateful. The less-than-happy news was the discovery of two plots to overthrow James. Both plots involved Catholic noblemen and underground Catholic priests. Sir Walter Raleigh was implicated by some of those arrested in the second plot, and although there was no corroborating evidence that he was involved, he was viciously attacked by the King's Attorney General, Sir Edward Coke. Raleigh was found guilty and sentenced to be executed, but King James would not sign the warrant for his execution. Raleigh was allowed to live under arrest in comfortable quarters in the Tower of London.

There were also rumblings of discontent from the Puritan party within the Church of England. The Puritans believed that the reformation of the Church of England had never been completed. They believed that the English church still had too many of the forms and ceremonies of the Catholic Church – symbols of theological positions that the Puritans rejected. The Puritans had presented a petition to James during his trip from Edinburgh to London in 1603. In 1604, he called for a conference at his palace of Hampton Court of the leading bishops and clergy of the Church of England. He also invited representatives of the Puritan faction to attend. During the course of the conference, James took the side of the Bishops on every point. He specifically rejected the Puritan proposal that the governance of the Church of England should be reformed and modeled on the Scottish practice of Presbyteries (representative assemblies of the clergy). "A Scottish Presbytery agrees with monarchy as well as God and the devil," he declared. He rejected the Puritan request that ministers be given some latitude in the way they conducted local services. "I will have one doctrine, one discipline, one religion, in substance and ceremony." When the Puritans objected that some of their clergy could not in good conscience use some of the Prayer Book ceremonies, he thundered, "I will make them conform or I will harry them out of this land, or else worse!" Only one of the Puritan suggestions did he endorse. He agreed that there should be a new translation of the Bible in English. But James added a condition. The new translation should include no marginal notes. James disliked the Geneva Bible, widely used in Scotland and by the English Puritans because of its marginal notes which criticized wicked kings and particularly the note which praised the Hebrew midwives for disobeying the command of Pharaoh. A committee of 47 scholars worked for the next seven years to review, revise, update and prepare the new translation. The first printed editions of the new Bible became available in 1611.

James' declaration that everyone in England should adopt "one doctrine, one discipline, one religion, in substance and ceremony," disappointed both the Puritans and the Catholics. A small but significant minority of the nobles in England had remained Catholic throughout the turbulent events of the reigns of Henry VIII, Edward VI, Mary, and Elizabeth. So long as they kept their religious views and practices private, they had, for the most part, been left undisturbed. The Catholic nobles had hoped for greater tolerance under James. Some of them now resolved that England could be returned to the Catholic fold if only they could overthrow the King. They conceived a fantastic plot to blow up the King and Parliament when they met in 1605. In the aftermath of the attack, the conspirators planned to raise a rebellion in the Midlands – the area of England north of London, and south of Scotland. Unfortunately for the plotters, the opening of Parliament was postponed several times. Though they managed to move 36 barrels of gunpowder into a storeroom they had rented under the Parliament building, the conspirators proved unable to keep a secret. At least one wrote a letter to a relative, warning him not to attend the opening session of Parliament. Guy Fawkes, the man in charge of the gunpowder was caught red-handed in the cellar, the night before Parliament was scheduled to assemble. He, and several dozen conspirators, including a Jesuit priest, were all tried for treason, convicted, and executed.

Here, a word must be said about the growing confidence and power of Parliament. Kings in England had been summoning Parliaments for advice and for the raising of funds for defense and war for several centuries. Parliament, especially the House of Commons, had steadily increased its right to control the financial affairs of the kingdom. Although the Parliament that met immediately after the discovery of the Gunpowder Plot was full of patriotic expressions of loyalty to the King, they refused to grant the King revenue and taxes for more than a limited time. This insured that the King would have to summon Parliament to meet again every few years. James found his financial dependence on Parliament maddening. It was humiliating for the King to have to beg for money from his subjects. James' first Parliament sat from 1604-1611. When it was dismissed, James resolved to govern without Parliament. He resorted to the sale of titles of nobility and other dubious measures. These measures raised some money, but not enough. In a few years, James was out of money. He reluctantly called for a new Parliament, but the House of Commons insisted on inquiring into the expenses of the King's household, and began a debate over the King's authority to impose taxes without Parliamentary consent. James became angry and dissolved Parliament only eight weeks after it had been convened. James then ruled for seven more years without calling Parliament into session again.

In 1612, tragedy struck King James and Queen Anne. Their 18-year-old-son, Henry, Prince of Wales suddenly became ill (probably with typhoid) and died. James and Anne had now lost five of their seven children. Only Charles, age 12, and Elizabeth, age 16 still survived.

The next year Elizabeth was married to a German prince, Frederick, the Elector of the Palatinate. After the wedding in London, Elizabeth left with her husband to take up residence at his court in Heidelberg.

Five years later, the Protestants in Bohemia began a rebellion against the Catholic Hapsburg Emperor and offered the position of King of Bohemia to Frederick. Frederick and Elizabeth accepted, and the young couple (they were both 22) journeyed to Prague to be crowned. The Habsburgs declared war, and one year later, Frederick and the Protestants in Bohemia were decisively defeated. Frederick and Elizabeth had to flee for their lives. At the same time, the Habsburgs invaded and occupied Frederick's Palatinate territories. Frederick and

George Villiers,
Duke of Buckingham

Elizabeth never returned to their court in Heidelberg. Eventually, they made their way to the Netherlands where they were given refuge.

One of the most astonishing events of James' reign as king was the rapid rise of a young man at court who became James' favorite and was the companion of the young Prince Charles. His name was George Villiers, and he was the son of a minor gentleman from Leicestershire. His father had died when he was 12 and his mother took great care to educate him for life as a courtier. He appeared at court in 1615, age 23, and was presented to James I, who immediately took a liking to him. James gave him a position at court and made him Viscount Villiers in 1616, Earl of Buckingham in 1617, Marquess of Buckingham in 1618, and Duke of Buckingham in 1623. In 1620, Buckingham married Lady Katherine Manners, the daughter of the Earl of Rutland. In addition to being highly favored by King James, he became the close friend of Prince Charles, who turned 21 in 1621.

Since 1614, King James had been actively negotiating with the Spanish ambassador for Prince Charles to marry the Spanish Princess, Maria. For King James, the proposed marriage had many advantages. He hoped it would secure long term peaceful relations between England and Spain. The Princess would also bring with her a huge dowry from the wealthy Spanish Court – money that James desperately needed since Parliament was being so stingy. But the proposed match was not popular with the English people. Parliament was summoned in 1621, ostensibly to raise funds for an English expedition to aid Elector Frederick and the Princess Elizabeth. But the members of Parliament reduced the amount the King requested and passed a petition to the King asking for Prince Charles to marry a Protestant. James reacted angrily and rebuked Parliament for interfering in matters of royal prerogative. Parliament responded by passing a statement protesting their rights, including a right in Parliament of freedom to debate any matter concerning the good England. King James dissolved Parliament and ripped the protest out of Parliament's record book.

Charles and Buckingham now decided to take matters into their own hands. In 1623, they traveled to Spain on their own under assumed names, hoping to woo the Princess Maria and conclude negotiations for the marriage. As it turned out, the Princess did not care for Charles and did not wish to marry a Protestant. The King of Spain informed Prince Charles and Buckingham that the Prince would have to agree to convert to Catholicism and pledge to repeal all of the anti-Catholic laws in England before the marriage could be agreed to. Charles and Buckingham gave up, and returned to England empty-handed. They were embarrassed, and angry at the Spanish court. They prevailed upon King James to summon Parliament once again. The English people were delighted and when Parliament was summoned in 1624, they quickly voted subsidies for a war with Spain. Charles and Buckingham opened negotiations with the court of Louis XIII, King of France and within a few weeks, Charles was engaged once again, this time to a French princess.

James was now 58 years old. Unfortunately, his health was not good. He had been King of England for twenty years, and King of Scotland for 57. In the first few months of 1625, he was frequently ill. In early March, he suffered a stroke which affected his speech and balance. A few weeks later, he died. He was widely mourned. Although the English had never completely accepted their Scottish King, they appreciated the fact that England had had relative peace for twenty years.

Much was expected of the young, 25-year-old prince, who now became King Charles I.

Matteo Ricci
Born in Italy, 1552 – Died in China, 1610

MAT THEVS RICCIVS MACERATENSIS QVI PRIMVS E SOCIETAE ESV E VANGELIVM IN SINAS INVEXIT OBIIT ANNO SALVTIS 1610 ÆTATIS 60

Macerata is a small town in northern Italy, about 180 miles north and west of Rome, on the Adriatic side of the Apennine Mountains, about 10 miles inland from the coast. It had been a part of the Papal States – the large expanse of territory in central Italy controlled by the Pope – since the early Middle Ages.

In 1552, Matteo Ricci was born there. His father was a pharmacist and the family was prosperous. At 16, Matteo was sent by his family to Rome to study law. Over the objections of his father, he left law school three years later and joined the Jesuits. The Jesuits had been founded in Paris in 1534 by Ignatius Loyola and six other students. The Jesuits called themselves the Company of Jesus and concentrated their efforts on three areas: founding schools and training students in classical studies and theology; missionary efforts to convert non-Christians to Christianity in the newly discovered non-European world; and to prevent any further spread of Protestantism. When Loyola died in 1556, the Jesuits were already operating a network of 74 colleges on three continents. In 1541, one of Loyola's original six companions, Francis Xavier, sailed from Lisbon to the Portuguese colony of Goa in India. After three years in Goa, Xavier began the first of 3 journeys further to the east, reaching both China and Japan in 1549. He died in Shangchuan, China in 1552.

After joining the Jesuits, young Matteo continued his studies. At the Jesuit college in Rome, he and his classmates went through a

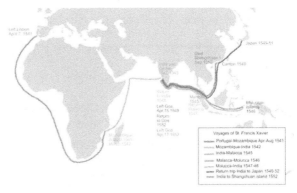

rigorous course of studies designed to prepare them for work in the mission field. Ricci's teachers included the German Jesuit mathematician Christopher Clavius, and the Italian Jesuit theologian Alessandro Valignano.

In 1573, Valignano was posted to the Portuguese colony of Goa by the Jesuits and placed in charge of all Jesuit missions in Asia. In 1577 he summoned his former pupil, Matteo Ricci to come from Rome and join the Jesuit mission to India. The work in India was progressing nicely. A far bigger challenge existed in China. The Emperor of China saw no reason to allow any foreigners into his kingdom. The Chinese people viewed all foreigners as barbarians. The tremendous difficulty Europeans faced in mastering the Chinese written language limited their effectiveness. Nonetheless, Valignano placed a high priority on the Jesuit efforts to reach China. In 1582, he transferred Ricci from Goa to Macao, a Portuguese colony on the cost of China, and assigned him the daunting task of learning the Chinese language.

Ricci proved himself to be a gifted student of languages. He made rapid progress in learning Chinese. After a year, Ricci moved from Macao to Zhaoqing in Guangdong Province across the bay. The significance of this move is that Ricci was no longer living in a European colony. Now he was living in a Chinese village. His language studies had progressed far enough that he was able to begin making his own translations into Chinese. His first efforts were the Ten Commandments, prayers, and a catechism, which he had printed so that he could use them with his first Chinese converts. For his Chinese friends, Ricci prepared a map of the world showing both China and the nations of Europe, as well as the newly discovered continents of North and South America. The map attracted a great deal of interest from the Chinese scholars in Guangdong Province. One scholar drew a copy of the map and had it reproduced by woodblock printing. Copies were sent to other scholars in other provinces, increasing the interest among the Chinese Mandarin class in this curious foreigner.

For ten years Ricci studied, preached, and cared for his growing flock of Chinese Christians in Zhaoqing. He, and a handful of Jesuits who had joined him, built a residence and a small church. But Ricci longed to reach the court of the Chinese Emperor, where he hoped to present the truths of Christianity and perhaps win the favor of the Emperor.

In 1595, Ricci set off on the long trip to the capital of China, Beijing – 1300 miles to the north. He reached Nanchang, about 500 miles from Zhaoqing, when he was forced to turn back by local officials who informed him that his permission to travel to Beijing had been revoked.

In 1598, he tried again. He managed to reach Beijing, but the imperial court was in an uproar over the Japanese invasion of Korea. The Chinese Emperor reacted by forbidding all contact with foreigners. Ricci was snubbed and ignored by everyone at court. After staying in Beijing for two months, he retreated south as far as Nanjing.

In 1601, Ricci returned to Beijing, this time for good. The Japanese scare had subsided. The Koreans, with assistance from the Chinese had defeated the Japanese. The mood at the Imperial Court was more open, more relaxed. Ricci brought with him a number of gifts for the Chinese Emperor, but the one which impressed him most was a clock. The Chinese still kept time by observing the movement of the sun and the stars and burning marked candles. The mechanical clock which the Jesuits had brought fascinated them. The Emperor gave orders that the western scholars were to be given a stipend and offered a place of residence within the Forbidden City. Although he was never permitted to see the Emperor himself, Ricci became the first European with access to the Chinese court.

For the next ten years, Ricci lived and worked in Beijing, in the Forbidden City. When he died in 1610, there were four small chapels in the Chinese Empire, each attached to a Jesuit residence – in Zhaoqing, Nanchang, Nanjing, and Beijing. There were several thousand Chinese Roman Catholics, many from the educated class. Ricci had also persuaded eight Chinese Christian converts to join the Jesuit Order.

He had also succeeded in introducing Christianity to the Imperial Court and the literary classes in China. He had translated key parts of the Bible into Chinese, and written some elegant tracts comparing the teachings of Christianity to the teachings of Confucius. The Chinese were impressed with this westerner who had spent so much time in learning their language and reading their classics and could write learned Chinese essays which matched the best writings of their own scholars.

Ricci, for his part, admired the Chinese. He wrote of them:

"of all the pagan sects known to Europe, I know of no people who fell into fewer errors in the early ages of their antiquity than did the Chinese. They began by worshipping Heaven (T'ien) and the Most High God (Shang-ti), and had no gods who were patrons of vices, unlike the Greeks, Romans, or Egyptians."

And although he may have never accomplished his goal of an audience with the Emperor himself, there is evidence that there were a number of Chinese Christians among the royal family when Ricci died. Christianity had taken root in China. Although the Chinese Christians would face many challenges over the next four centuries, their numbers would continue to grow. By the year 2000, there were many millions of Chinese Christians.

William Shakespeare
1564-1616

William Shakespeare was born in the village of Stratford-upon-Avon in 1564. We do not know anything about what sort of schooling he may have received. When he was 18, he married Anne Hathaway, age 26. The Shakespeares had three children. Daughter Susanna was born in 1583, when William was 19 and Anne was 27. Twins Hamnet and Judith were born two years later in 1585.

After the birth of his three children, there are no records that tell us what William was doing for the next seven years. He may have been a country schoolmaster. And although we have no records of his own schooling, the plays that he wrote demonstrate that Shakespeare was very well read in the classics and understood both Latin and French.

Sometime between age 21 and age 28, Shakespeare moved from Stratford to London and pursued a career in the theater – first as an actor and then later as a playwright. By the time he was 28, we know that several of his plays were being performed on the stage. Some of the other London playwrights complained about the upstart Shakespeare. They had all been educated at the universities of Oxford and Cambridge. Although Shakespeare was their equal in creativity and command of the language, he had no university degree.

We know that by 1594, when he was 30, Shakespeare had joined an acting company called the Lord Chamberlain's Men where he continued as an actor and as a writer of plays. The Lord Chamberlain's Men performed their plays mostly in rented halls. They were popular at the court of Queen Elizabeth and several times a year were invited to stage their performances in one of the monarch's castles for an audience composed of the Queen and the nobility of

England. In 1599, the Lord Chamberlain's Men raised enough money to purchase a plot of land on the south bank of the Thames, just across the river from the city of London, where they built a permanent theater which was called the Globe. From 1599 on, this was where all of Shakespeare's plays were staged. The Lord Chamberlain's Men remained popular with Queen Elizabeth and were even more popular with King James after 1603, when he became their sponsor and they changed the name of their company to The King's Men. The sale of tickets for plays at the Globe made all the members of the company tidy profits. Shakespeare made annual trips to Stratford-upon-Avon and spent several weeks each summer visiting his wife and children. He invested his share of the profits from the Lord Chamberlain's Men/King's Men by buying property in Stratford – moving his family into the second-largest house in town in 1605.

Over the course of 21 years, Shakespeare wrote some 38 plays, 154 sonnets, and two long narrative poems. His plays have been translated into almost every language on earth and are still performed more often than those of any other playwright. They are generally divided into comedies, histories, and tragedies. About half of them were published during his life. In 1623, seven years after he died, a collection of 36 of his plays was published which scholars now refer to as the First Folio.

In these plays, Shakespeare shows himself to be a genius of the theatre and a skilled observer of human nature – both its admirable qualities and its failings. He generally wrote some two or three new plays each year for The King's Players. 1599 was perhaps his greatest year. To help draw audiences to the newly opened Globe, Shakespeare completed and the company premiered four new plays: **As You Like It** (a comedy about love, against a backdrop of political exile in which three couples exhibit three different styles of wooing); **Julius Caesar** (which culminates in the assassination of the Roman leader and the impassioned speech over his corpse by Mark Anthony); **Henry V** (a historical retelling of the great English national hero and his conquest of France against overwhelming odds); and **Hamlet** (perhaps the most famous and oft-quoted of Shakespeare's plays, about the struggle of the Prince of Denmark to avenge the murder of his father by his uncle).

In 1623, when the First Folio collection of his plays was published, his contemporary and rival playwright Ben Jonson wrote an introductory poem praising Shakespeare. Among the lines he penned are these:

Soul of the age!

The applause! delight! the wonder of our stage!

[. . .]

Triumph, my Britain; thou hast one to show

To whom all scenes of Europe homage owe.

He was not of an age, but for all time!

[...]

Sweet swan of Avon, what a sight it were

To see thee in our waters yet appear,

And make those flights upon the banks of Thames

That so did take Eliza and our James!

But stay; I see thee in the hemisphere

Advanced and made a constellation there!

Shine forth, thou star of poets, and with rage

Or influence chide or cheer the drooping stage,

Which, since thy flight from hence, hath mourned like night,

And despairs day, but for thy volume's light.

John Smith

1580-1631

Born in January of 1580, John Smith's life can be divided into three chapters. As a young man, he was a widely travelled soldier of fortune. In his late 20s and 30s, he was a founding colonist and later President of the English Colony of Virginia. After that, he was, by commission from the king, a sea-captain and Admiral of New England. He was also an author who gave us a vivid first-person account of his far-ranging adventures. Of most historical significance, it was Smith who insured that the colonists in Jamestown, Virginia survived their first few difficult years, and it was Smith who coined the name "New England" for the northeastern coastal area of North America.

John Smith was born on the farm his parents rented at Willoughby, near Alford, Lincolnshire near the eastern coast of England, about 140 miles north of London. Though his family were tenant farmers, they were not poor. John attended the local schools, and at 15 was apprenticed as a clerk to a merchant in the nearby town of Lynn. But the life of a clerk did not appeal to John at all. As a young man, his imagination had been captured by the stories of the voyages of Sir Francis Drake around the world, and the adventures of Sir Walter Raleigh, battling Spanish galleons in the new world and attempting (unsuccessfully) to plant a permanent English colony there. Above all else, the defeat of the Spanish Armada in 1588, when John was eight years old, thrilled him. Along the English coast, only a few miles from his parents' farm, signal fires had been lit to track and warn all those along the coast as the Armada sailed by.

When John Smith's father died in 1596 (it seems his mother had died earlier, though we don't know exactly when), he inherited a small amount of land and some livestock. These he immediately sold and set off to see the world. He traveled first to France, first to Paris, and then to the channel port of Havre. There he joined a company of English soldiers under the command of Captain Joseph Duxbury. For the next three years, John served as a soldier with the English forces in the Netherlands, alongside the Dutch Protestants who were fighting for independence from Catholic Spain. When his term of enlistment was up, John sailed for Scotland. The ship carrying him was sunk in a storm (the first of many misfortunes at sea), but John managed to reach Edinburgh and the court of King James. Without any ready money, or a source of income, he found securing any position in Scotland difficult. After a few months John returned to his home in Willoughby.

Back home, his friends and neighbors were much amused by his behavior. The restless youth who wanted to run away to be an explorer like Drake and Raleigh was now a sturdy young man, with three years of military service to his credit. He spent the summer reading Marcus Aurelius and Machiavelli and practicing his riding and swordsmanship. But he remained restless, and resolved to travel abroad once again – this time even further afield. He decided he would journey through Europe to the eastern frontier of Christendom where the armies of the Holy Roman Emperor were fighting desperate battles to keep the Turks at bay.

Of course, the trip from England to Austria was an adventure in itself. John had one misfortune after another. His possessions were stolen from him in France by rogues who pretended to have befriended him. When he finally reached the Mediterranean and embarked on a ship bound for the east, he found himself caught in a tremendous storm. The passengers and crew of the ship decided that John Smith was the cause of the foul weather. They cursed him for being both a Protestant and an Englishman, and threw him overboard. John managed to swim to the shore of a nearby island, and within a day or so was recruited to join the crew of a passing Breton ship which had also been caught in the storm. They sailed first to Alexandria, Egypt and after landing a cargo there, doubled back for the Adriatic where the captain decided to engage in a bit of privateering (attacking other ships at sea and stealing their cargo). The captain seized a rich Venetian merchant ship, and John Smith's share of the cargo made him (temporarily) a wealthy young man. His share of the loot amounted to perhaps 50,000 dollars (adjusted for 2009).

With money in his pocket, John decided to enjoy himself and visit the historical cities of the Ancient Roman Empire. He visited both Florence and Rome, and after six months as a tourist, he resumed his journey towards Austria where he joined the Imperial army. In his first action, he proved his worth by devising a trick with a string of fireworks that distracted the Turkish soldiers besieging an Austrian town. Smith was promoted and made commander of a cavalry troop of 250 men. Quite an honor for a young Englishman just recently turned 21!

Over the next two years, John led his troop of horseman bravely in a number of engagements. His bravery and skill as a leader became well known throughout the Emperor's army. In 1602, during a long siege of the town of Reigall, one of the besieged Turkish warriors offered a challenge to single-combat to any officer of the Emperor's army who dared accept. Smith accepted, and killed the Turk at the first pass in a joust. One of the Turk's friends then challenged Smith to a second combat. He was likewise killed by Smith. When a third Turkish champion challenged Smith, he too was dispatched.

When Prince Sigismund of the Imperial Army heard of Captain John Smith's exploits, he knighted him, promoted him to Major, and presented him with a coat of arms displaying three Turk's heads. It took John Smith twenty years to get around to registering his title with the Heralds' College back in England, but the commission is still there, complete with Prince Sigismund's seal and signature.

The war with the Turks continued. Major Smith and his cavalry troop continued to serve with distinction. But in 1602, the Imperial army that Smith was serving with was suddenly surrounded, outnumbered, and defeated by a force of 40,000 Tartars. Smith was wounded and left for dead on the battlefield. The next day, he was discovered alive by scavengers on the battlefield, taken prisoner, and sold into slavery. A Turkish nobleman bought him and sent him to Constantinople as a gift to his betrothed, a Greek princess named Charatza Tragabigzanda, who was still living with her family.

Of course, she fell in love with John.

She was worried that her mother might sell John to an evil master, so she made arrangements for him to be sent to her older brother who was a local official for the Turks in a territory on the far side of the Black Sea. She hoped that John would return to her in a few years.

Charatza's brother proved to be a tyrant and a scoundrel. He owned hundreds of slaves, and treated them all badly. He was furious at the idea that this English slave might have won his sister's heart. Within an hour of his arrival, he had Smith stripped, clothed in a hair coat, and riveted a heavy iron collar around his neck. John Smith was now thousands of miles from home, a slave, held deep in the steppes of central Asia, north and east of the Black Sea.

John Smith had been a slave for some months when, one day during the harvest, his cruel master approached him in the barn where he was threshing grain and began to beat him. John Smith could endure it no longer. He turned and attacked the cruel master with his threshing club and killed him. He then fled, dressed in his master's clothes and riding his master's horse, but with the hated iron collar still on his neck.

For sixteen days, John Smith rode north and west towards the closest Christian outpost he knew of, in Russia. At last, he reached safety. As soon as he explained himself to the commander of the Russian garrison, he was welcomed, given new clothes, and released from his iron collar. It took several months for him to make his way from one Russian garrison to the next back to the Imperial Army in Austria. His old comrades in the army welcomed him with surprise and joy. He was rewarded with a handsome sum by the delighted Prince Sigismund, and when he expressed a desire to return to England, sent on his way with letters of introduction and a parting bonus. Of course, John had a few adventures on his journey back to England, including a raging 3-day battle at sea with two Spanish galleons, but after shipwreck, privateering, duels, battles, and escaping from slavery, the details are hardly worth mentioning.

Thus ended chapter one in John Smith's life. He was now 24 years old and a military veteran. He had fought with an English company against the Spanish in the Netherlands. He had served at sea with a Breton crew and captured a Venetian merchant ship. He had fought in the Austrian army against the Turks, and he had been captured, sold into slavery, and then escaped and returned home.

And what was a young man with such wide and varied military experience to do next in life? It will surprise no one that he was drawn into the company of men who were preparing a second attempt to plant an English colony in the New World. King James had granted a charter to a company of wealthy gentlemen in London with the right to start a colony. The backers included men who had been veteran explorers of the Atlantic and not a few who had fought the Spanish Armada back in 1588. The company outfitted three ships and dispatched them with 105 colonists for the coast of North America in 1607. Among those on board was John Smith, now 27 years old.

In April, 1607, the little fleet entered Chesapeake Bay. Within a day or so, the ships had discovered the mouth of the James River and proceeded to sail further upstream to the north and the west. The water remained calm and deep and as the river narrowed, the ruling council selected a site for their colony. Captain Newport negotiated an agreement with a local Indian chief and, in exchange for an axe-head, the Indians agreed that the colonists could build a village of their own.

John Smith should have been a part of the ruling council, but he wasn't. Its members had been kept secret until the expedition reached Virginia. When the letters naming the council members were opened, John Smith was a prisoner in irons, still on board ship. He had quarreled with some of the highborn noblemen on the voyage and the Captain had had him arrested on a charge of mutiny. The quarrel may not have been as serious as it seemed in the middle of the ocean - for after a few weeks in Virginia, John Smith was released and joined the colonists on shore.

One of the first tasks of the colonists was to explore the river and see how far west it might go. Some of the explorers speculated that the North American continent might be only a hundred miles or so wide and that the river might lead them through to the Pacific Ocean. It took only a few days of sailing in the colonists' small boat to reach the rapids of the James close to the location of the modern city of Richmond. The explorers raised a cross on an island in the river in view of the rapids with an inscription claiming the territory for King James of England. This was to be the western limit of European settlement in Virginia for the next 50 years.

The explorers made contact with small groups of Indians wherever they went. None of the tribes was large, 30-60 warriors in each separate group as near as they could tell, but it was difficult to discern their intentions. At times they seemed friendly; at times they tried to steal from the colonists; at times they seemed belligerent and intent on picking a fight.

The English nobleman who had been elected President of the governing council, Edward Wingfield was unsure about what steps to take. John Smith urged that the colonists construct a palisade fort as quickly as possible, in order to be able to defend themselves against attack. Wingfield decided not to. He did not want to "antagonize" the Indians. He dismissed Smith's concerns as those of a hot-headed, low-born adventurer. He and the other proper English gentlemen were sure they could maintain good relations with the Indians. John Smith was but a hot-headed youth. Let older, wiser, and cooler heads prevail.

A few weeks later, two hundred Indians suddenly rushed out of the woods and attacked the camp of the 100 Englishmen. There was a short sharp struggle. The sailors on board the ships quickly began firing the ships' cannons over the head of the attacking Indians and they retreated back into the woods. But two Englishmen had been killed and a dozen wounded. President Wingfield suffered the indignity of having an Indian arrow pass through his beard.

Suddenly, John Smith's advice seemed quite prudent, and the colonists quickly began building a fort – a 3-sided wooden palisade. Smith's exclusion from the ruling council was also re-considered, and he was invited to take his place among the other gentlemen.

A few weeks later, the three ships which had brought them departed for England. Within a few days, many of the colonists were sick or dying. The heat of coastal Virginia was oppressive to those used to the milder climate of England. There were fevers and diseases and there was a shortage of food. President Wingfield was dismissed by the council, and John Ratcliffe chosen as the new president of the colony. Ratcliffe immediately appointed Smith as superintendant of the colonies food supplies and delegated to him responsibility for all trading with the Indians.

The Englishmen continued to fare badly. Most of the food they had brought with them from England was gone. The caught fish and gathered berries, but they were reluctant to venture too far from the fort and hunt game for fear of being attacked by Indians. Within six weeks of the departure of the ships back to England, 51 of the 105 colonists had died. The colonists had arrived too late to plant and harvest any crops. Young Captain John Smith organized, cajoled, and shamed the surviving colonists into finishing the buildings in their settlement and to gather and store as much food as possible for the coming winter. He traded for grain and other food with the Indians whenever the opportunity arose.

In December, with winter about to begin, Smith took nine other colonists out to explore further up the Chickahominy River in hopes of finding more supplies. The voyage quickly took a tragic turn. Smith's party was ambushed by Indians and the other nine were all killed. Smith was taken prisoner and carried to the village of Powhatan, chief of all the Indian tribes in coastal Virginia. Powhatan was a stern chieftain and a great warrior. He did his best to intimidate Captain Smith with a display of 200 warriors and challenged Smith to explain why the English were building a permanent village and why they had traveled so far up the rivers which emptied into Chesapeake Bay.

Powhatan seems to have known that the number of English warriors had dwindled from over a hundred to less than fifty. After talking with the other chiefs and the leading braves, he decided that John Smith must die. As the warriors stretched John Smith out on a broad flat rock and prepared to smash his head with their clubs, Powhatan's ten-year-old daughter suddenly

 darted out of the crowd and threw herself down on top of Smith. She laid her head on his and hugged it with her arms. The warriors could not strike Smith without harming the chief's daughter. She pled with her father to spare the life of this strange white man. Powhatan had to relent. He informed Captain Smith that he was free, and an honored friend of the Powhatan Indians. He sent him back to the settlement at Jamestown and requested that Smith send gifts to the Indians – Chief Powhatan particularly wanted one of the large English stones they used to grind corn into flour and also a cannon.

Captain Smith smiled graciously, agreed to be friends with Chief Powhatan and his braves and made his way back to Jamestown, escorted by 12 Indian warriors and gifts of food for the other Englishmen. It had been a month since he had left on an expedition to find food.

The surviving colonists were desperate for food and supplies. The food sent by Powhatan was most welcome. Captain Smith shrewdly offered to give the 12 warriors one of the cannon to take back to Powhatan, but when they tried to lift it, they found it much too heavy to carry (as Smith had known they would).

A week later, Pocahontas and several warriors appeared outside the fort with more food for the Englishmen. Over the next few weeks, Pocahontas visited several more times, each time with more food. Without the food they provided the remaining colonists might have starved.

A few weeks later Captain Newport arrived back from England with more supplies and a hundred more colonists. The survival of the colony now seemed less doubtful.

In the spring, Captain Smith felt confident enough in the condition of the settlement at Jamestown to embark on two lengthy voyages of exploration of all of Chesapeake Bay. He traveled several hundred miles north, exploring each river as he encountered it, making maps and charts of the areas which would in the future be home to the cities and towns of Yorktown, Alexandria, Baltimore, and Philadelphia. His maps and charts have proven so accurate that historians have been able to confidently establish his course on modern maps. During these voyages, Smith and the twelve soldiers he took with him had numerous encounters and adventures with the Indian tribes who roamed the shores of the bay. They were attacked half a dozen times, but used their muskets and pistols to surprise and shock the Indians and ward off each attack. At other times, they were able to meet peacefully with groups of Indians and trade with them and question them about the rivers and pathways of the bay.

John Smith was now elected president of the colony – the third president of Virginia – and set about organizing the new settlers for the coming winter. Their food situation was better than the year before, but they would still need to trade with the Indians. A far larger problem was the reluctance of many of the new colonists to do any hard work. They had heard tales of the Spanish explorers finding rich veins of silver and gold and seemed to think they could prosper in the new world with little or no effort. Smith told them bluntly that they must join the others and work each day to build their own houses for the winter and to strengthen the palisade walls which protected Jamestown. If they did not work, then they would not eat. Smith would share none of the food supplies with lazy gentlemen who thought they might find gold and silver lying on the ground.

Through the second winter, the settlement fared much better. Only seven colonists died during the second winter, in contrast to the fifty who had died during the first. As Captain John Smith finished his one year term as president of the colony, he was injured in a terrible accident.

He was asleep in the bottom of a boat returning down the James River when a spark ignited a bag of gunpowder that he had been lying against. He was horribly burned and at first his friends thought he might die. He survived, but his wounds would not heal properly. So, in December 1609, nearly three years after he and the other colonists had arrived, Captain John Smith was carried aboard a ship bound for England – where he hoped he might find a doctor who could heal his wounds. When he left Virginia, thanks to the several voyages made each year by Captain Newport, the little colony at Jamestown had grown to almost 500 men. They were healthy, they had planted and harvested enough food to feed everyone through the winter, and they had 60 hogs and 500 chickens. It seemed certain that the settlement would survive.

In fact, within the next six months Jamestown came close to being wiped out. With Smith gone, there was a lack of sound leadership. The Indians had feared and respected Smith. When they heard he was no longer at Jamestown, they became bolder and more belligerent. The inhabitants of Jamestown at first feasted on their stores and slaughtered their livestock and chickens. When food began to run short, they attempted to trade with the Indians. The Indians refused, and instead ambushed and killed English settlers whenever they could. By spring only 60 of the 500 settlers were still alive. When an English ship arrived, they begged to be taken back to England.

John Smith's crossing of the Atlantic was swift and without incident. With the aid of skilful doctors back in England, he was restored to health, though for a long time he was quite weak. Tales of his adventures spread throughout England and his name was soon a household word. There were even performances on the stages in London in which his rescue by the Indian princess Pocahontas were acted out – to great applause by the crowds.

John heard the news of the tragic "Starving Time" which had nearly destroyed Jamestown and begged the Virginia Company in London to give him a commission to sail back and relieve the colony. His request was turned down.

He prepared a detailed map based on his exploration of Chesapeake Bay and had it published along with an essay he had written describing the Virginia colony and the Indian tribes who inhabited its river valleys.

He also met with the great English explorer Henry Hudson, who had been employed by the Dutch to explore the coast of North America and stake a claim for their colony of New Amsterdam – on a little island near the mouth of the great Hudson River, which he had discovered. Hudson left Smith the draft of a map which showed a stretch of coastline almost two hundred miles long between the Dutch claim and the French claim further to the north.

Smith resolved at once to return to North American and explore this coast in detail and to claim it for England. He secured financing from some friendly London investors and in the spring of 1614, he sailed for the northern coast of the New World in command of two ships. This was not an attempt to establish a colony. The purpose was to explore, prepare detailed maps, and if possible make a modest profit by fishing, whaling and trading for furs with the Indians.

Captain John Smith's six month voyage of 1614 was a success. He left England in March and returned in August. During those months he had made detailed maps, identified a number of likely spots where good anchorages and fresh water could be found (both essential for the site of a permanent settlement) and his men had filled the holds of the two ships with fish and furs. They showed an unexpected profit for the investors.

Smith was anxious to sail again. He prepared a detailed map, giving names to prominent features along the coast – including Cape Tragabigzanda, named after the Greek princess who had befriended him while he was a slave in Constantinople. He called the stretch of North American coastline that he had mapped "New England." In the fall of 1614, he took his maps to Prince Charles, now heir to the throne and the young prince agreed to sponsor further voyages, and to assist in the planting of a second English colony on this more Northern Coast. He disliked some of the names on Captain Smith's map though, and changed them. Thus we know the peninsula north of Boston as Cape Ann rather than as Cape Tragabigzanda.

In March of 1615, Smith set sail from England again, but this year he had bad luck. His two ships were both badly damaged in a storm. Running back to port in England, he transferred to a smaller ship and resolved to try crossing the Atlantic again. He fought one engagement with English pirates, and then ran into a French fleet which seized his ship and placed him under arrest. Smith protested that he was no pirate, but sailed with a commission from the King of England. But his crew proved treacherous, and they slipped away from the French fleet and sailed back to England, leaving Smith stranded as a prisoner on a French warship.

The French commander offered Smith a position as master-gunner of the warship. Smith agreed with the condition that the French would, at the end of their voyage, set him ashore on the Azores or allow him to transfer to any ship bound for England which they might encounter. For the rest of that year, Smith sailed with the French warship as an officer and master-gunner. Smith distinguished himself in a score of engagements with Spanish and Portuguese ships. When the sailing season was at an end he begged the French captain to honor his bargain, but was refused. As the ships approached the coast of France, a storm sprang up and with most of the crew below-decks, Smith launched one of the ships boats and escaped. After a terrible ordeal in the storm, his small boat was washed up on the coast of France. He later learned that the ship he had escaped from had sunk in the storm with the captain and most of the crew drowned.

Smith made his way back to England, and at once set to work organizing another expedition for the spring of the next year, 1616. But that winter he had an unexpected visitor – Pocahontas, the Indian princess, now married to one of the Virginia colonists, John Rolfe, and a baptized Christian with the new name of Rebecca. She was in England and wished to see him. It was an emotional reunion. For a time, Pocahontas was unable to speak, overcome by emotion. But when she could, she thanked John Smith and called him "father." He in turn, gave her thanks for having saved his live in that terrible winter eight years before. Sadly, Rebecca died that same winter, without ever being able to return to her native Virginia.

Just as sadly, Captain Smith never reached New England again either. A fleet was gathered and provisioned in the spring of 1616 but remained becalmed in Plymouth harbor all spring. The voyage had to be abandoned. John Smith was now 36. Not nearly old enough to retire, but he found he was no longer called upon to lead ships and settlers. Instead, he wrote books. He wrote on shipbuilding and on pirates. He wrote a history of his travels and adventures. And he kept writing and lobbying all who would listen that England should establish more settlements in the New World. Smith's books and pamphlets were widely read, especially his description of New England based upon his voyage of exploration along the coast in 1614.

In the spring of 1620, Captain Smith learned that an attempt to establish another colony in the New World was being organized in London on behalf of a group of religious separatists known as "Pilgrims." He offered to lead the expedition. The Pilgrims politely declined, but thanked him for the books and maps which he had written. They had no money to pay him, and they did not quite trust the soldier-captain who did not share any of their religious convictions.

Captain Smith was disappointed. When he later heard reports of the terrible experiences of the Pilgrims, half of whom perished in the first winter, he was dismayed. His experience might have spared them much suffering. But as the second English colony in the new world took hold and began to flourish, he was pleased. He was also often consulted by the London Virginia Company. When word reached London in 1622 that the Indians had staged another attack upon the colony in Virginia and killed over 300 settlers, Captain John Smith offered to lead an expedition of reinforcements to defend the colony. As plans were being made for that voyage, it was discovered that the Virginia Company was bankrupt and had no funds. The settlers in Virginia were on their own.

Smith continued to live in London. He had many friends, including other English soldiers who had fought with him against the Turks and settlers, sailors, and soldiers who had sailed with him to the new world. In 1629, four years into the reign of Charles I, a group of Puritans resolved to plant their own colony in New England. They consulted Captain Smith, but at 49, he felt he was not up to the rigors of pioneering a new settlement on the coast of the new world. Instead, he wrote a book for the guidance of the colonists which they much valued. If the new colony prospered, he thought he might perhaps join them once it was well-established.

But it was not to be. In 1631, at the age of 51, he suddenly took ill and died just a few days later.

He had often spoken of Virginia and New England as his children:

"I may call them my children, for they have been my wife, my hawks, my hounds, my cards, my dice, and in total my best content, as indifferent to my heart as my right hand to my left."

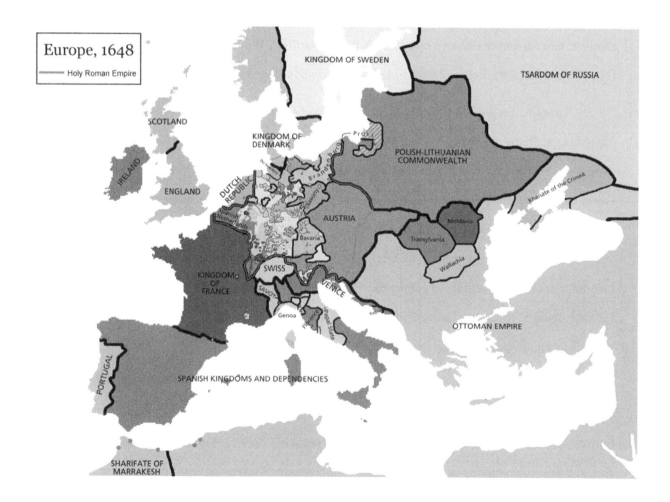

Albrecht von Wallenstein

1583–1634

A bloody religious war broke out in Germany in 1618, and, as it lasted until 1648, it is called "The Thirty Years' War." This war was one of the most dreadful that ever raged in Europe. It was a struggle between the Catholic and Protestant parties in Germany, like that in France which we have read about in the story of Catherine de' Medici and Henry of Navarre.

Many Catholics and Protestants opposed each other because they wished to defend their belief as well as to convert others to it. But many of the German princes and nobles used the disturbed religious conditions to increase their power. Thus religion and politics were mingled and confused. The two great parties of the war were known as the Catholic League and the Evangelical Union. All through those thirty years the Catholics and the Protestants of Germany strove with all their might to overcome and destroy one another.

Of course this great war brought forth great leaders. The ablest general on the Catholic side was Albrecht von Wallenstein, who was born in Bohemia in 1583. His parents were Protestants. They died while he was yet a child; and he was brought up by an uncle who was a Catholic. This uncle sent him for his early education to the Jesuit College at Olmutz, and afterwards to the universities of Bologna and Padua. While at the Jesuit College, Wallenstein became a Catholic, and this changed his whole career.

From his father Wallenstein inherited a large estate and an immense sum of money. By his marriage with an aged widow his wealth was nearly doubled; and when his uncle died and left him his property, Wallenstein became one of the richest men of his day.

His aged wife did not live long after their marriage, and he took for his second wife a daughter of the Count of Harrach. By this second marriage his wealth was again increased; and through his wife's father, he gained much influence and many friends at the court of Vienna.

After completing his education he traveled through Italy, Spain, France, and Holland. He served for a short time in Hungary in the army of the Emperor Rudolf who was then at war with the Turks. But as yet he did not display any marked ability as a soldier.

With a part of his wealth he purchased from the emperor of Austria a vast territory in Bohemia and Moravia, at a cost of over seven million florins. To this territory he gave the name of Friedland, that is, Land of Peace.

The emperor gave him the title of Duke of Friedland and he managed his duchy wisely and well. Justice was so faithfully administered in the courts that all men had their rights; and the farmers, miners, and manufacturers were properly cared for.

When the "Thirty Years' War" broke out Wallenstein raised a regiment of dragoons to aid the cause of the emperor. He was also the means of saving the money in the imperial treasury from falling into the hands of the enemy.

As Wallenstein came more fully into notice his ambition steadily increased. In all that he did, he seemed to have an eye to his own advantage.

After the war had been going on for some time, the emperor found himself sorely in need of a better army. Then Wallenstein called upon him and said, "My liege, you shall have such an army as you require. I myself will bear the expense of equipping it. I make, however, this condition, that I shall have the right to compel the people in any part of the empire where my troops may be fighting to supply them with provisions;" and to this condition the emperor agreed.

Wallenstein soon made for himself a reputation as a great commander. There were plenty of men in Germany who were ready to fight for pay and plunder, and he soon raised a force of over thirty thousand soldiers. He himself went with them to the front.

During the first two years Wallenstein and his men were everywhere successful, but at length they met with a severe check. They had laid siege to a large commercial city called Stralsund. This was one of the wealthiest ports on the Baltic. It exported a great deal of grain and other produce, and vessels flying its flag were seen in every harbor of Europe.

Wallenstein determined to capture Stralsund. His soldiers knew that if he succeeded, they would get a vast amount of plunder, and an abundance of provisions for their future use.

Wallenstein had more in mind than that. He planned to turn the merchant vessels of Stralsund into battle ships, and thus secure a fleet which would enable him to carry on the war by sea as well as by land. He would then attack the other great ports of Germany, such as Lubeck, Hamburg and Bremen.

All these ports had large fleets of merchant ships. He planned that after taking these he would make his navy the largest in the world. He even dreamed of capturing the ships of England, Sweden, and the Netherlands, and thus making himself master of the sea.

It was with these thoughts in his mind that Wallenstein laid siege to the great port of Stralsund. He swore that he would capture it "even if he found it to be fastened to heaven with chains of gold."

But Stralsund was well supplied with provisions; and, for eleven weeks, the brave citizens repelled his attacks. Wallenstein's men began to suffer for lack of food; and at last the great commander was forced to abandon the siege.

Every year a festival of rejoicing is still held in Stralsund to commemorate the day on which Wallenstein and his starving army retreated, baffled and angry, from before its walls.

Wallenstein had won so many victories that some of those who fought on his side had become jealous of him. As soon, therefore, as he met with this great reverse at Stralsund, his enemies persuaded the emperor to take the command of the army away from him.

They made the emperor believe that he was a very dangerous man, and that with his large army which had grown very fond of him, he meant to rule all Germany, and lord it over every prince and duke in the empire.

The emperor at once wrote him a letter ordering him to give up his command. Although greatly surprised, Wallenstein took his dismissal in silence. He bade farewell to his troops, and went to live quietly in the capital of his duchy.

Not long after Wallenstein had left the army the emperor found that he had made a mistake. Instead of hearing of victory after victory, he now received news of one defeat after another. His second-best general was fatally wounded; and he had no one like Wallenstein to put in command of the army.

After suffering a number of disastrous defeats the emperor sent to Wallenstein and begged him to take command once more. He gave him permission to choose his own officers, and to carry on the war just as he thought best. He also promised that, in future, no one should interfere with him.

On these terms Wallenstein again accepted the emperor's offer, and was soon back in the field at the head of an army of forty thousand men.

By this time, however, a greater general than even Wallenstein had become the leader of the Protestant forces. This was the famous Gustavus Adolphus, king of Sweden, whose bravery had already been shown on many a bloody field.

The two commanders and their armies met near a place called Lutzen, in Saxony, and there a fearful battle was fought. In this battle Gustavus lost his life, but his army fought on nobly and won the day. The victory at Lutzen is always spoken of as the greatest victory of the "Thirty Years' War."

When Wallenstein found that the Protestant army had won the battle in spite of the loss of its commander, he became greatly troubled, and scarcely knew what to do. He seemed afraid to meet such an army again. He doubtless saw that it was useless to continue the war, and hoped that the emperor would make terms to the Protestants, and so establish peace.

Wallenstein's enemies again appeared before the emperor with the old story that he was simply fighting for himself, and was determined to make himself ruler over the entire nation. Strange as it may seem, the emperor again believed them. He even went so far as to call Wallenstein a traitor, and he caused him to be publicly disgraced and again removed from command.

With a guard of about a thousand men, and accompanied by several of his leading officers, Wallenstein left the camp and once more started for his home. He supposed that all who accompanied him were his faithful friends. But it was not so. Four of the men whom he thus trusted had already agreed to assassinate him. Having first murdered his real friends, they hurried to the house where Wallenstein was staying, broke into his room, and killed him as he was retiring to rest. It is said that, for this shocking crime, the murderers were handsomely rewarded by the emperor.

Wallenstein ranks as one of the world's greatest military commanders. His betrayal by the emperor he served is a sobering reminder that loyalty is not always returned or rewarded by those who hold high office.

Gustavus Adolphus

1594–1632

In the year 1594 a child was born in the royal palace of Stockholm who was destined to have great influence upon the history of modern Europe. He was the son of Charles IX, king of Sweden, and a grandson of the famous hero, Gustavus Vasa. He was given the name of Gustavus Adolphus.

As soon as he was old enough to begin his education he was provided with the best of teachers. He soon learned to speak Latin, Greek, German, Dutch, French, and Italian. Gustavus was also carefully instructed in athletics, especially in riding, fencing, and military drill. He was a boy of muscle as well as of mind, and he soon proved the value of both. Before he was eighteen his studies were brought to an end by the death of his father. He was at once proclaimed king of Sweden.

At the time of his father's death, Sweden was at war with Denmark. The Danes had captured the two most important fortresses of Sweden. Gustavus was determined to win them back, and he took command of the Swedish army with the intent to use it against the Danes.

A few months after his accession the Danes sent a fleet of thirty-six ships against Stockholm, but Gustavus, marching night and day, led his army to a point from which he could attack the Danish fleet with advantage. A storm also hindered the Danes from landing, and they returned home disappointed.

When the king of Denmark heard of these rapid marches, and found that he had no mere boy to contend with, he consented to a treaty of peace by which Sweden regained one of her fortresses and was permitted to buy back the other.

From 1614 to 1617, Gustavus was at war with Russia to recover the pay due to Swedish soldiers which his father had sent to Russia a few years before.

In that war he took from Russia the two provinces of Carelia and Ingria. These provinces remained in the possession of Sweden for more than a hundred years, serving as a great barrier between Russia and the Baltic Sea. Even the land on which St. Petersburg now stands passed into the hands of the Swedes; and at the close of the war, Gustavus declared, "The enemy cannot now launch a boat on the Baltic without our permission."

When Gustavus came to the throne, Sweden was at war also with Poland. The cause of the war was this: Charles IX, the father of Gustavus, was not the true heir to the Swedish crown. It belonged, by right, to Sigismund, king of Poland. Sigismund had been King of Sweden and had led the Swedish armies in a war of conquest against Poland. He sought to rule both countries, but the nobles of Sweden had no wish to be ruled by an absentee king. When Gustavus was only a year old, the Swedish parliament had deposed Sigismund and given the crown to his uncle, Gustavus' father, Charles IX.

Sigismund wanted the crown of Sweden back. He had tried to take it from Charles; and he now tried to take it from Gustavus. But Gustavus won a great victory over Sigismund and forced him to abandon his claim to the throne and to make a peace which was of great advantage to Sweden.

Ten years before the birth of Gustavus a new star had suddenly appeared in the northern skies of Europe; and people thought that wonders in the heavens had much to do with events upon the earth. The new star rapidly became one of the brightest in the firmament. It could be seen by men with keen eyes even in the day time. But it soon began to lose its brilliancy, and in about a year and a half it disappeared entirely.

When Gustavus Adolphus startled Europe by his brilliant victories over Denmark, Russia, and Poland, men began to believe that the wonderful star foreshadowed the wonderful boy king of Sweden. Some, however, began to speak of him as the snow king, and declared that he would soon melt. Finally, they came to think of him rather as one of the old Scandinavian war gods, and they found that he was equal to greater tasks than those he had already accomplished.

The empire of Germany was, at that time, divided against itself. The "Thirty Years' War" was raging. The grain fields were trampled down by marching troops. Towns were besieged and burned. Innocent people were destroyed by thousands. Two great generals, leading the Catholic armies of the Emperor — Wallenstein and Tilly — were filling the empire with horrors.

In 1631 the Protestant city of Magdeburg was taken by Tilly. Its little garrison of twenty-four hundred men had made a noble defense, but Tilly had no respect for their bravery. As soon as the city fell into his hands he put these brave soldiers to death. During the next two days his soldiers pillaged the city and slaughtered more than twenty thousand of the inhabitants.

All Europe was horrified. The Protestant princes and nobles of Germany begged the Protestant King of Sweden to come to their aid. Gustavus Adolphus gathered an army of thirteen thousand chosen men and at once invaded Saxony.

On the outskirts of the little town of Breitenfeld, not far from Leipzig, Gustavus met the inhuman Tilly and defeated him in battle.

The people of Saxony were wild with delight. They gladly opened the gates of their cities to welcome the conqueror of the dreaded Tilly. The German Protestant nobles now had a general to rally behind. They flocked to the standard of Gustavus and his army was soon more than four times as large as when he had left Sweden.

With this large body of fresh troops at his command, Gustavus determined to follow the Catholic German army which had retreated into Bavaria.

Having overtaken the Catholics, he at once put his army into line and began the attack. In the desperate battle which ensued Tilly was mortally wounded; and he died as he was being carried from the field.

It was at this time that the Catholic Emperor recalled Wallenstein and again placed him in command of the German army, as we have read in the previous story.

It was not long before Gustavus and Wallenstein found themselves face to face upon the field of combat. They met in battle near Lützen, in Saxony, to which place Gustavus had returned on account of the large number of Saxons in his army.

During the morning a thick fog hung over the field and the fighting did not begin until nearly noon. Then, as the skies cleared, the king and his army approached the Catholic lines singing Luther's hymn, "A mighty fortress is our God." As they ceased singing, Gustavus waved his sword above his head and cried, "Forward! In God's name," and the battle began.

In one particular Gustavus was most imprudent. A wound, received some time before, made it painful for him to wear a breastplate; and so he led his troops into the engagement, wearing a common riding coat. Early in the afternoon his arm was pierced by a ball from a pistol, and this probably severed an artery.

For a time he concealed his wound and continued to encourage his men. But he grew faint from loss of blood, and finally said to one of the princes riding near him, "Cousin, lead me out of this tumult. I am hurt."

As they turned, a musket ball struck the king in the back, and he fell to the ground dying.

Some of Wallenstein's men rode up and inquired his name. "I am Sweden's king," he replied. "I am sealing the religion and the liberty of the German nation with my blood."

When told of the death of the king, the second in command of the Protestant army is reported to have exclaimed, "There is still time to make a good retreat." The German Duke of Weimar turned on him angrily and replied, "There is still time to win a glorious victory!"

When the troops of Gustavus learned of his death, they attacked the enemy with such fury that Wallenstein was quickly defeated. Gustavus had won the battle although he lost his life. Suddenly the star in the north had become the most brilliant in the heavens; and as suddenly its light was quenched. The snow king had melted at last.

But a great work had been done. Gustavus and his brave band of Swedes had inspired half a continent with hope and courage. His splendid victories also did much to crush the tyrannical power of the Catholic Emperor in Germany; and the good which this great man accomplished has had much to do with the spreading of religious liberty over Europe.

After the battle was over, and just as twilight was gathering, the body of the hero was carried into a little church nearby, and laid before the altar. The soldiers, still dressed in their armor, were the chief mourners; and a village schoolmaster read the simple service for the dead.

Next morning the body was embalmed, and then carried to the nearby city of Wittenberg where is lay in state in the town church where Luther had preached. When the German Lutherans had honored the great Lutheran general of the north, Swedish soldiers took the body back to Stockholm. There it was laid to rest in the church of Riddarholm which contains the royal tombs, and where many others of the greatest and best men of Sweden are buried.

Samuel de Champlain
1570-1635

Samuel de Champlain was born in the French port city of Brouage on the Bay of Biscay. Historians think he was most likely born in the year 1570, but they are not sure. Although Champlain wrote numerous books and essays about his explorations in the New World, he wrote very little about himself. We know only a few things about his family. Most everyone in Brouage made their living by some connection with the sea. They fished and harvested salt from the sea, or they worked as ship captains and crew, or they were merchants who bought and sold cargoes from around the world. Champlain's father seems to have begun his life as a local sailor, then worked as a pilot – a special navigator who helped larger ships navigate the dangerous passageways through the sandbars and into the harbor – and finally as a ship captain himself.

We do not know the details of Champlain's youth and education. From his later writing there is evidence that he, much like Shakespeare, had attended and done well at the basic subjects in school, but had "little Latin and less Greek."

Champlain grew up in the decades of the French religious wars, which lasted from 1562 to 1598. He was, probably, about 24 years old when Henry IV was crowned King in the Cathedral of Chartres. Champlain and all his family were passionate supporters of Henry of Navarre. Both his father and his uncle received commissions from King Henry IV as ship captains in the Royal Navy of France. The first official records we have of Samuel de Champlain tell of his service as a soldier with Henry IV during his campaign to drive the Spanish out of Brittany. The Spanish had intervened in France as allies of the Guise family's Catholic League. The records show that

Champlain began as an ordinary soldier, but was steadily promoted. He became an aide to the highest ranking marshals of the army and ended the campaign as the commander of a company. It was a remarkable record for a young man in his twenties, who had not been born to nobility.

The campaign in Brittany was the last phase of the Religious Wars in France. In May of 1598, Henry IV successfully concluded negotiations and a peace treaty between France and Spain was signed at the town of Vervins. All Spanish troops were withdrawn from France. The French Catholic League, which had refused to recognize Henry IV as king ended their opposition to his rule.

The end of fighting in France presented new opportunities to Champlain. The army raised for the war in Brittany was disbanded, and he was honorably discharged from service, with the thanks of the King. Champlain did not want to go home to Brouage. He wanted to widen his horizons. His imagination had been captured by accounts of the New World, across the ocean, on the continents of North and South America. The Spanish had discovered it first, and by 1598 they had their own thriving settlements from Mexico City south to Santiago in Chile. Both the French and the English had also sent explorers across the Atlantic, and had staked claims in the New World. But in 1598 neither country had been successful in establishing any permanent colony there.

Champlain resolved to embark on his own voyage of exploration – not in command of a ship – but as a passenger with the Spanish. There is the possibility that he had been commissioned by King Henry IV as a spy to gather information on the Spanish settlements in the New World. Champlain himself wrote:

> ". . . I resolved, so as not to remain idle, to find means to make a voyage to Spain, and, being there, . . . to embark in some one of the ships of the fleet which the king of Spain sends every year to the West Indies; to the end that I might be able there to make inquiries into particulars of which no Frenchmen have succeeded in obtaining cognizance, because they have no free access there, in order to make true report of them to his Majesty [King Henry IV] on my return."[1]

---

[1] **The Works of Samuel de Champlain**, Toronto: Champlain Society, 1922-1936, volume 1, pp 5-6. A Digital version of the entire six volumes is available online at the website of the Champlain Society, www.champlainsociety.ca

Champlain succeeded in this improbable quest, traveling with the Spanish fleet in February of 1599 to San Juan, Havana, Porto Bello, Cartagena, and Vera Cruz. While in Vera Cruz, he managed to travel overland to Mexico City, where he estimated the population to be 12,000-15,000 Spaniards and perhaps another 70,000 Indians. In the fall of 1600, he returned with that year's Spanish fleet to Spain, and then made his way back to France. He wrote a detailed account of his voyage to the Spanish settlements in the New World (which included 62 carefully hand-drawn maps of harbors and fortifications) and seems to have had no trouble securing an audience with King Henry IV and presented his report in person.

The King responded by awarding Champlain an annual pension and directing him to remain at the court. Champlain used his time to make a careful study of the records of previous French attempts to establish settlements in the New World. It is clear that he was already making plans to establish a French colony in the New World. There had been several previous attempts by the French, and they had all failed. The locations had all been poorly chosen and the settlers had never been given sufficient supplies. The religious divisions between Protestants and Catholics had played a part as well.

In 1602, King Henry IV commissioned a French nobleman, Aymar de Chaste, as the royal governor of New France. De Chaste was a veteran soldier of the Religious Wars, a loyal supporter of King Henry IV, and Vice Admiral of the Royal Navy. De Chaste set about organizing a great voyage of exploration and settlement. Three ships were hired, and outfitted with everything thought necessary. Champlain was asked to join the expedition. De Chaste was elderly and not in good health. He appointed Captain Francois Grave, sieur du Pont (referred to as Pont-Grave) to command the expedition and recommended Champlain to him as an able assistant. Champlain also carried a letter of recommendation directly from King Henry IV which appointed him as the King's personal observer. In 1603, the French squadron of three ships set sail for the New World.

After a voyage of six weeks, the ships entered the St. Lawrence river, one hundred miles wide at its mouth and sailed west towards its northern bank, and then south west towards the interior. By chance, the French ships happened upon a gathering of Indians along the banks of the Saguenay River where it joined the St. Lawrence near Tadoussac harbor. Over a thousand Algonquin Indians from a dozen tribes had gathered to celebrate a recent victory over their rival tribes to the south, the Iroquois. Champlain and Pont-Grave decided to seize the opportunity. Accompanied by two Indian interpreters they had brought with them from France, they crossed the water in a small boat and walked bravely into the midst of the Indian camp.

It was a tense moment. Pont-Grave and Champlain could not be sure that they would be welcomed by the Indians. The two French leaders were taken to meet the Anadabijou, Chief of the Algonquin and seated in a place of honor. Their Indian interpreters explained to the chief that the two Frenchmen were representatives of the great chief or King of the French nation across the ocean. The Indian interpreters said they had been treated well by the French (they had volunteered to sail back to France with French fisherman several years before) and described for the chief the great size of the French cities and the strength of the French castles.

Chief Anadabijou listened to all the Indian interpreters said, then he passed a pipe of tobacco to Pont-Grave and to Champlain and then to his principle warriors. After a pause, he said: "I am pleased that the King of the French should want to send his people to live in this place with us, and to make war with us upon our enemies."

With the friendship of the Indians assured, Pont-Grave and Champlain spent the rest of the summer exploring the St. Lawrence valley, looking for a suitable place for a permanent settlement. Further upstream, where the river narrowed, Champlain found what he thought was an ideal spot. After a summer exploring and mapping the rivers and tributaries of the St. Lawrence valley, the French expedition sailed down the St. Lawrence and crossed the Atlantic back to France. This time Champlain did more than just write a report for the king. He wrote a book describing his voyage, the riches of the St. Lawrence valley, and all the "true wonders" of the new world. His book was published only eight weeks after he returned to France.

Champlain was saddened to learn that Admiral Aymar de Chaste had died while he was in the New World. He hurried to Paris to make his report to King Henry IV and to do all he could to make sure the King appointed someone to take de Chaste's place who would be equally supportive of the vision of establishing a permanent French settlement in North America. Just six weeks after Champlain's return, King Henry IV appointed Pierre Dugua sieur de Mons as the new "vice admiral for all the seas, coasts, islands, harbors, and maritime countries which are found in the said province and region of Acadia." De Mons was a close friend of the King's. He favored a permanent French settlement in the New World. Champlain tried to persuade him to select the location he had identified at the narrowing of the St. Lawrence, but De Mons had other ideas. He wanted an outpost on the Atlantic, closer to France, somewhere along the coast of Newfoundland, a region the French called L'acadie – later known as Acadia. De Mons was to have command of the expedition and the settlement. He invited Champlain, as the king's cartographer, to accompany him. Champlain readily agreed.

De Mons outfitted two ships, loaded them with supplies, and recruited settlers. The expedition seems to have numbered about 120 – all men. At first the colony was to be a quasi-military outpost. Families would have to come later. In April of 1604, the two ships sailed from France for the New World and arrived four weeks later off the coast of Acadia. De Mons and Champlain spent several weeks exploring the coast looking for a suitable site for a settlement. They finally settled upon Sainte-Croix Island. The island in June looked lush, green, and inviting, while at the same time having features which would make it easy to defend in case of attack by Indians, or (more likely) by other European ships. De Mons and Champlain supervised the construction of buildings for the settlement – a storehouse, barracks, and bunkhouses. In September, the two ships sailed back to France, leaving seventy-nine men to spend the winter in New France. Then things began to go horribly wrong. The island of Sainte-Croix is at almost the same latitude as Brouage in France (in fact, it is a little south), and so the settlers expected the winter to be much as it was at home. When it began snowing in October the settlers were shocked. When the water around the island froze solid in December they were alarmed. The actions of the tides in the bay kept the ice around the island in a jumble of weird broken shapes. They could not get their boat through to the mainland, neither was the ice solid enough to cross on foot. The settlers quickly ran short of firewood, and then began to run low on food. They had expected to be able to hunt to supplement their stores. That was now impossible. In January the settlers started to die. By the time the supply ships arrived in May from France, thirty-five of the seventy-nine settlers had died, and most of the survivors were very ill – from malnutrition and scurvy. De Mons and Champlain realized they had made a terrible mistake in selecting the island as the site for their colony. All the survivors were loaded on board the supply ships and sailed across the Bay of Fundy to a new site, and a new settlement was begun at a protected bay named Port Royal.

While the new settlement at Port Royal was being built, De Mons and Champlain used the spring and summer of 1605 to explore further south down the coast. They carefully explored the several hundred mile long coast of what is now Maine and charted Massachusetts Bay and Cape Cod. Along the coast of the Cape, a French shore party was accosted by a party of Indians. The French had no way to communicate with them, as their language was totally different from the northern Algonquin tribes. A scuffle broke out and a French sailor was killed. The Frenchmen fired their muskets at the Indians, without any discernible effect other than to cause them to break and run away. Although the climate promised to be milder than the site in Acadia, De Mons concluded that a settlement here would be too risky, facing the hostility of the Indians. De Mons and Champlain turned their boat around and sailed back to Port Royal. De Mons returned to France at the end of the summer. Champlain elected to stay over the winter in the New World with the other settlers at Port Royal.

The winter was not as severe as it had been at Sainte Croix Island, but it was still a difficult fight for survival. Twelve of the forty-five colonists died of scurvy and malnutrition. As the winter slowly came to an end, the colonists watched anxiously for the spring supply ships from France. They were late. Champlain had hoped to see them in May, or at the latest, before the end of June. By the first of July all of the settlements stocks of food were gone, and the situation looked grim. They had not established any system of agriculture which could support the settlers over a second winter without more supplies from France. On July 17th, the surviving colonists abandoned Port Royal and sailed around the southern cape of Acadia and up along the Atlantic coast, hoping to encounter a French fishing vessel which could take them all back to France. When they finally did spot the sails of a ship, it was the overdue French supply ship, with a new governor (the sieur de Poutrincourt) and fifty new settlers. The survivors were taken aboard and everyone sailed back to the Port Royal.

For several months both newcomers and veterans worked to improve the buildings and to plant and tend vegetable gardens. In late summer, Champlain and Poutrincourt embarked on another voyage to the south to explore the coast. On Cape Cod, once again, a shore party was attacked by Indians, with four sailors killed and several more wounded. The French once more turned around and sailed North, concluding that the hostility of the Indians made a settlement anywhere on Massachusetts Bay or Cape Cod impractical. By November, all the French were back at Port Royal, some preparing for their second winter in the New World.

The second winter went better than the first. They were better supplied this year than they had been the previous one. They were more prepared for the cold. They organized more frequent hunting for fresh game and had better success. Early in the spring of 1607 (just as John Smith and the members of the Virginia Company were sailing into Chesapeake Bay), the supply ship from France arrived to find the colonists in much better shape than the previous year. But they brought bad news from France. The company which had been given a commission by King Henry IV to plant a settlement in the New World had gone bankrupt and the King had withdrawn its commission and monopolies. The ship's captain was under orders to evacuate all of the settlers from Port Royal and bring them home to France. And so, after one winter at Sainte Croix Island, and two winters at Port Royal, Champlain and the other settlers abandoned the French settlements in Acadia.

Champlain did not give up his dream. He went to work with his old friend and ally, de Mons. By January of 1608, they had persuaded the King to renew the commission to plant a colony in New France, and to renew the monopoly on the fur trade to provide funds for the colony.

In the spring of 1608, Champlain returned to New France. It was at least his fourth voyage across the Atlantic. He had already spent the better part of three years exploring and, more importantly surviving the brutally cold winters. This time, he was no longer just a cartographer or the King's observer. Now he was to be in charge of the settlement. He and de Mons had recruited colonists and bought supplies. More importantly, Champlain had persuaded de Mons that the new settlement should be planted in the St. Lawrence River valley, rather than on the harsher Atlantic coasts of Acadia.

Champlain led his colonists across the Atlantic and up the St. Lawrence to the place where the river narrowed, a place he had explored five years before. The Indians called it *kebec*. Champlain declared it to be the perfect spot for the French outpost that would govern New France.

Beginning on that summer day in 1608, Champlain devoted the next twenty-seven years to organizing, promoting, and strengthening the settlement of Quebec and the development of New France. Things got off to a rocky start. Only twenty-eight settlers started the winter of 1608-09 at the small collection of buildings called the Habitation de Quebec. When spring finally arrived in 1609, twenty of the twenty-eight had died. The re-supply ship from France arrived the first week of June. It brought only eight new settlers – but that doubled the population! That number would be temporarily increased by the number of sailors and soldiers who had come across the Atlantic with the ships – though they would be sailing back again in the fall. While he had a larger number of Frenchmen with him, Champlain had a bold plan.

For some time, Champlain had been aware that an ongoing state of war existed between two larger groupings of Indian tribes in the northeastern forests of North America: the

Algonquin tribes, who lived in the valley of the St. Lawrence and the territory to the north, and the Iroquois tribes who lived to the south in what is now upstate New York and along the southern shores of Lake Ontario. The Algonquin Indians in the valley had repeatedly stressed that they desired the French to join with them in defending their settlements against attacks and raids by the Iroquois. Champlain now agreed to take twenty men with him and join the Algonquin warriors in an attack into the heart of Iroquois territory, against the Mohawk tribe. In June of 1609, he left Quebec and sailed up the St. Lawrence, along with several hundred Algonquin warriors. Several weeks later, they reached the mouth of what the Algonquin called the "Iroquois River" (today's Richelieu River) which flows from south to north, where it joins the St. Lawrence. Traveling up the river, they would be heading into the heart of Iroquois territory. After travelling about 30 miles south, they came to rapids in the river which forced them to abandon the larger French boat. All but two of his French companions decided to turn back towards Quebec. Champlain, his two French companions, and about sixty Algonquin braves continued south. In a few days, they reached a large, narrow lake which was the source of the river. The scenery around the lake was (and is) spectacular. The lake itself was only a few miles wide, but was 125 miles long, stretching far to the south. As his band of Algonquin warriors traveled cautiously south, they were constantly on the lookout for Iroquois. At the south end of the Lake they found them. In Indian fashion, the two parties agreed to meet for battle on shore the following morning. When the two parties of warriors faced each other in a clearing at the edge of the lake, Champlain, by prearrangement, suddenly stepped out of the Algonquin ranks, advanced, strode forward about 60 feet in front of his own ranks. Almost midway between the two groups of Indians, he leveled his arquebus, aimed, and fired. His first shot killed three of the Iroquois leaders. When his two French companions (who had slipped quietly around to the flank of the Iroquois party) also opened fire, killing several more, the Iroquois broke and fled. The Algonquin chased them into the woods and killed several dozen and took a dozen prisoners. The Algonquin were ecstatic at such a stunning victory over their enemies. Always before, the Iroquois had been the aggressors, raiding the Algonquin territory, burning their villages, and taking captives back to their lands. Now the Algonquin, with the help of Champlain, they had turned the tables.

After this successful voyage (which for Champlain was a combination of exploration and military expedition), Champlain returned to Quebec, issued final instructions to the settlers for the coming winter, and boarded the ship sailing back to France. In October, less than three months after his discovery of Lake Champlain, and successful raid against the Iroquois, he was standing before King Henry IV at the palace of Fontainebleau making a full report about few developments in New France.

Six months later, he turned around and made the crossing back to New France and to the Habitation de Quebec. To his delight, the winter had been mild and all the settlers had survived. After a brief stay in Quebec, he sailed further up the St. Lawrence to the "Iroquois River." While underway, he was met by a party of Algonquin in a canoe who urged him to come with them quickly. They had trapped a war-party of about 100 Iroquois warriors in the woods near the river. Champlain and the Frenchmen with him hurried to the scene and joined in the fighting. At the end of the day, the Mohawk had been annihilated. 80 had been killed in the fighting. The Algonquin promptly tortured and executed the 12 prisoners. For the next twenty years, no Iroquois raiding party ventured into the lands of the Algonquin again.

Champlain returned to Quebec and spent the summer organizing and supervising improvements and expansions to the buildings and the cultivation of larger fields. He was at Quebec in late summer when the shocking news arrived from France that King Henry IV had been assassinated. Champlain quickly gave instructions to the settlers for the coming winter and returned to France. The new king was Louis XIII, nine years old. Until he was older, the government was in the hands of his mother, Marie de' Medici. The Queen mother had little interest in New France. Still, Champlain was able to organize the supply ship for the following spring and returned to Quebec, anxious to find out how the settlers had fared over the winter. Once again the settlers had survived with no losses. For the next twenty years, with few exceptions, this was the pattern Champlain followed. In the spring, he would sail to Quebec with a supply ship and new colonists. He would spend the summer exploring the interior of New France and in the fall take ship back across the Atlantic. In 1613, he published **The Voyages of Champlain, Captain to the King** which contained three large maps of New France. He dedicated the book to King Louis XIII and his mother, Marie de' Medici.

In 1628, tensions between England and France erupted into a brief war, fought mainly at sea, after the English sent troops in an attempt to break the siege of the Huguenots in La Rochelle. In the summer of 1628, a squadron of six English ships under the command of the Kirke family (father and five sons) sailed into the St. Lawrence and demanded the surrender of Quebec. Champlain refused, but faced desperate straits with no supply ships from France able to get through. He had 90-100 settlers in Quebec to care for and not nearly enough food. He sought help from the surrounding Indians, but it was a difficult winter for the French settlers. In the summer of 1629, the Kirkes returned, and having learned of Quebec's desperate shortage of food, once again demanded that it be surrendered. Champlain had little choice but to comply. The Kirkes agreed to transport all of the French settlers across the Atlantic to England and to arrange for their return to France. When Champlain arrived in England, he learned that a peace treaty had been signed before he had surrendered Quebec and that the treaty obligated the English to return any settlements of New France that they had occupied. He stayed in England for several months attempting to secure the return of Quebec, but eventually gave up and returned to France. Back in France, he devoted all of his energy to stiffen the resolve of King Louis XIII to demand that the English honor the terms of the treaty. King Louis XIII's sister, Henrietta Maria had married King Charles I in 1625. Charles insisted that before he returned New France to French control, the French finish paying the dowry of several million dollars. Finally, Richelieu and the King agreed to make the promised payment to the English, and the English agreed to return Quebec.

In the spring of 1633, Champlain set sail for New France in order to take charge of the territory once again as the King's Lieutenant General in New France. When he arrived in the St.

Lawrence valley, he was pleased and surprised to discover that the English had already evacuated and that French settlers (who had been taken in by the Indian tribes) and already resumed control of the habitation de Quebec. Many of the buildings were in ruins. The English had not taken very good care of things. Perhaps they knew (or suspected) that they would not be staying for long. Champlain went immediately to work, cleaning, clearing, repairing, and beginning several important new buildings. Among these was a chapel, which he named Notre-Dame-de-la-Recouvrance, in honor of the restoration of New France.

The Indians were happy to have Champlain back. The English had not treated them well. One of the Huron chiefs made a speech to welcome Champlain.

> "When the French were absent, the earth was no longer the earth, the river was no longer the river, the sky was no longer the sky. But on the return of the sieur de Champlain everything was as before; the earth was again the earth; the river was again the river, and the sky was again the sky."

For the next few years, Champlain oversaw the restoration of New France. He had brought 150 settlers with him in 1633. 200 more came in 1634, and a further 300 in 1635. For the first time, there were women and children among the settlers. The little settlement at Quebec expanded rapidly, as did the establishment of farmsteads in the surrounding countryside. The settlement of New France seemed at last to have taken root and begun to grow. In only a few years they were no longer dependent for food on annual supply ships from France. In the fall of 1635, Champlain suffered a stroke which left him partially paralyzed. He died on Dec 25th, 1635 in Quebec, at the age of 65. At his funeral, the French inhabitants of Quebec, along with hundreds of Indians from all the Algonquin tribes marched in procession to honor him.

Altogether he had made 27 crossings of the Atlantic from France to the New World over the course of thirty-seven years. It is a remarkable and noteworthy fact that he never lost a ship.

Galileo Galilei

1564-1642

In the year 1583, repairs were going on in the cathedral of the old Italian city called Pisa. A workman had accidently set swinging a great lamp which was suspended from the high roof of the building. People came into the church and knelt for a few minutes to say their prayers and then went out without noticing that the lamp kept on swinging to and fro.

A young man about eighteen years of age came into the church. He noticed the swinging lamp. He watched it for a while and it occurred to him that it took just the same time to make each of its swings. He watched for a while to see if the time of each swing was getting slower. It seemed to remain constant.

With his right hand he clasped his left wrist. He knew that the times between pulse beats are practically equal. So, feeling his pulse and watching the swinging lamp, he was trying to measure the one by the other.

The young man who watched the swinging lamp was Galileo. By simple observation, he had made one of the great discoveries in the field of physics – that the swing of a pendulum remained constant, even as the distance that it swung grew smaller.

Before his time no pendulum had ever swung in a clock. No clock with a pendulum had been thought of. But after Galileo published his great discovery that pendulums made their swings in equal periods of time, a man named Huygens made a pendulum clock.

It was found that pendulums about a yard long make each swing in a second; and so, at first, clocks were made with pendulums which beat seconds. From Galileo's watching the swinging lamp, all our clocks may fairly be said to have been invented.

The father of Galileo had hoped that his son would become a physician; but the young man liked to study mathematics, and his father permitted him to follow the bent of his genius.

Not long after graduating at the university, and when not quite twenty-five, Galileo was made professor of physics. He taught his classes about pumps and machinery, why smoke rises in the air, why birds' wings enable them to fly, and why fishes' fins send them through the water. All that anybody in Europe at that time knew much about such matters were the writings of ancient Greek philosophers, primarily Aristotle. ——> knowledge based mainly on Aristotle

People had made very little study about such simple things as the falling of stones and feathers, and pieces of iron and lead. Even learned men thought that two pounds of lead would fall twice as fast as one pound, one hundred pounds one hundred times as fast – because Aristotle said so in his writings. One day Galileo asked some of his friends to climb with him the leaning tower of Pisa. This tower is one of the famous buildings of Europe.

Some of Galileo's friends stayed at the foot of the tower; some went to the top. Heavy and light things were carried up and dropped from the summit of the tower; and one pound of iron reached the ground at the same instant as did a piece that weighed ten pounds. Thus Galileo refuted Aristotle and promoted the practices of observation and experimentation – the foundations of modern scientific study.

While Galileo was professor at Pisa the people of Europe who watched the heavens saw a new star in the sky.

"Have you seen the new star? What do you think it is?" were questions that everybody was asking. Some thought it was only a meteor; but Galileo said, "No! It must be a star, because a meteor would surely be moving, and that star seems still." He began to give public lectures upon it and people went by hundreds to hear him.

Galileo, like everybody else, could look at the star only with the naked eye. He tried to contrive something that would show both it and the other stars more plainly. He had seen spectacles. His grandfather wore a pair. He had somewhere read that if two eyeglasses are placed one above the other, things seen through them will appear nearer and larger.

Hans Lippershay in Holland had fixed an eyeglass at one end of a tube and another like it at the other end; and so made the first telescope. Galileo had heard about this. He bought a piece of lead pipe and fixed a glass at either end. His telescope magnified only three times; but it made things look nearer and larger.

He was as pleased with it as a child with a new toy. Wealthy and noble Italians looked through it with wonder; just as when you look through a microscope at the point of a needle you are surprised to see how blunt it is.

Then Galileo used stronger lenses. His second telescope magnified eight times; and a third was made which magnified thirty times.

He looked at the moon; and he saw what no human being had ever seen before. There are mountains on the moon. He saw their bright tops and the shadows which they threw.

Then he looked at the planet Venus. She no longer looked like the other stars; but sometimes she seemed to be round like the full moon, sometimes horned, like the old and new moons.

With his naked eye Galileo counted only six stars in the Pleiades. People long years before had seen seven; and it was believed that one had been lost. Galileo looked one bright night and his telescope showed him forty. He looked at the Milky Way and found that its whiteness is the dim light of millions of stars so far away that they seem as small as the finest dust.

He then made a fourth and larger telescope, and turned it upon the farthest away of the known planets. Jupiter, like Venus, seemed no more a star. It was round like the moon at the full.

But another and greater wonder appeared. Close to the edge of Jupiter's disk were three tiny stars. Two were seen on the east side of the planet and one on the west. They were Jupiter's moons. Galileo watched on another night and found that instead of three there were four. We now know that there are seven.

He told the other professors in the university what he had seen, and the news quickly spread. The newly-found moons were called planets, just as our own moon was; and so it seemed that Galileo had made the number of planets eleven, instead of seven.

Not all the professors believed Galileo's report. One of the professors was so angry that he would not even look through the telescope. Another man said, "The head has only seven openings—two eyes, two ears, two nostrils and one mouth, and how can there be more than seven planets?"

Galileo had an old friend called Kepler, who was the greatest astronomer then living. Galileo wrote to him, "Oh, my dear Kepler, how I wish we could have one good laugh together. Why are you not here? What shouts of laughter we should have at their glorious folly!"

About sixty years before this, Copernicus had printed a book in which he said that the earth was not still, as people thought, but that it was all the time moving round the sun.

Galileo did not at first believe this, and said in one of his letters that it was "folly." Then he saw that it was probably true. When he looked through his telescope at the planets he became certain of it.

When people said that the system of Copernicus was contrary to the teaching of the Scriptures, Galileo tried to explain that the passages in the Bible which describe the sun rising and setting are to be taken only as descriptions of what men saw. He was then accused of teaching what would do harm to religion, and was summoned to Rome His trial took place in 1616 and he promised to give up his opinions concerning the Copernican system and not to teach or promote it.

But his enemies still pursued him. In 1633 Galileo was again accused of heresy and of breaking the promise he had made in 1616. The main part of the charge was that Galileo had denied that God is a personal being and that miracles are not miracles at all. As to breaking the promise he had made in 1616, Galileo admitted that he had felt proud of his arguments in favor of the Copernican system and in one of his books he had made out rather a strong case for it. He denied, however, having expressly taught the Copernican system. Unfortunately Galileo did not tell the truth in thus denying what he had taught, and he was sentenced to an indefinite term of imprisonment.

The imprisonment was not severe, although Galileo complained of it. He was to remain with an old friend and disciple; but at the end of six months he was permitted to return to his home near Florence. His friends were allowed to visit him; but he was not allowed to go outside the gate to visit them. This was sad for him; but sadder still was the loss of his sight; for his eyes had seen more of the glory of the heavens than all the millions of eyes that had ever looked at the stars since the world began.

He died in 1642 and his body was interred in the Cathedral of Santa Croce.

Cardinal Richelieu

1585–1642

While Wallenstein on the one side, and Gustavus Adolphus on the other, were fighting the battles of the "Thirty Years' War" in Germany, the religious tensions in France resulted in civil war once again. Louis XIII and his famous prime minister, Richelieu, were fighting with the Huguenots, or Protestants of France.

Louis sat on the throne, but the real ruler of France was Cardinal Richelieu. The full name of the Cardinal was Armand Jean du Plessis de Richelieu. Richelieu was the name of his father's estate, upon which, in 1585, Armand was born.

When he was twenty-two he entered the ministry and soon became a bishop. His people were mostly poor. Richelieu felt that there was a grander career before him than to remain their bishop. He determined to make something of himself, and to be the equal of any nobleman in the kingdom. There was only one way in which he could do this. That was by becoming a politician. His ambition was to become a leader of men.

In Richelieu's time, there was an assembly in France called the states-general. It was composed of delegates who represented the nobles, the clergy, and the commons—the three great classes into which the nation was divided.

But the states-general had no real power. It did not, like the US congress or the English Parliament, make laws. It could only petition the king. The delegates presented addresses to His Majesty, telling him of any trouble in the kingdom and begging him to remedy it.

Richelieu, being a bishop, was a member of the states-general, and although he was one of the youngest—perhaps the very youngest of the bishops—he got himself chosen as the orator who should deliver the address of the clergy.

This gave him a good opportunity to win the favor of Louis XIII's mother, the famous Marie de Medici, widow of King Henry IV, who was acting as regent of the kingdom until Louis should come of age. Richelieu praised her extravagantly in his address, and she naturally took a liking to him.

About a year after his oration at the meeting of the states-general, Richelieu was invited by the queen mother to become a member of the council, as Secretary of State, with responsibility for foreign affairs. He time in the council, however, was only short-lived. Louis turned 16 in 1617, and was determined to take power back from his mother and rule in his own name. The young King and his friends resented Marie de' Medici and her chief advisor, Concino Concini who were both Italians. In April, 1617 Concini was assassinated on the orders of Louis XIII and Marie de' Medici was ordered to retire from the court to her country estate at Blois. Richelieu's resignation was accepted and he departed Paris and returned to his country estates.

Two years later, Marie escaped from her confinement at Blois. King Louis called Richelieu to court to assist him in negotiating with his mother. Richelieu was able to secure the reconciliation of the King with his mother and was asked by the King to remain in Paris at the court. In 1622, King Louis nominated Richelieu for a cardinal's hat, which the Pope granted. Shortly thereafter he was appointed the King's principal minister and became the most valuable officer that Louis ever had.

When King Henry IV of Navarre had granted to the Huguenots the celebrated Edict of Nantes, the French people generally hoped that the religious troubles in France were forever ended. But unfortunately, this was not the case. In 1621 some of the Huguenots held a great meeting at La Rochelle, which was their richest city, and there made a kind of declaration of independence.

The king of France had several fortresses in that part of the country. One of these, called "St. Louis," commanded La Rochelle.

King Louis considered that he had a right to maintain fortresses anywhere in France, but the Huguenots insisted that the fortress of St. Louis should be demolished. The king, instead of pulling it down, made it stronger. The Huguenots then did a very unwise thing. In 1622 they rose in a general revolt, and made an attack on some of the king's war vessels and captured them. Richelieu, however, managed to put down the revolt.

Two years later the English made war upon France and again the Huguenots revolted. Richelieu then decided that their power must be destroyed. With an army of twenty-five thousand men he marched to La Rochelle and besieged it. The city was well protected. On the land side were vast swamps through which an army could neither march nor drag siege guns. An attack might have been made by sea, but at that time the king had no navy.

To prevent food being taken into the city across the marshes was easy; but the only way to prevent its going in by ships was to close the harbor. To do this, a great stone dike, a mile long, was built across the channel that led to the city.

Richelieu paid his men twice ordinary wages, and in that way, although it was winter, he succeeded in getting the work done. The harbor was thus closed. Food soon became scarce, and great suffering prevailed in La Rochelle.

But no one thought of surrender. The women were just as determined to hold out as were the men. Months passed, and still the siege went on. The starving citizens hoped every day to see an English fleet come to their aid. An English fleet did come, in the spring of 1628. But when the English commander learned of the great dike that Richelieu had built, he was afraid to approach it lest his ships should be wrecked. He therefore sailed away without firing a gun.

At the close of the summer the besieged were obliged to eat horses, dogs, and cats. It is said, that they boiled the skins of these animals, and even boiled old leather trying to make it fit for food.

In September of 1628 a second English fleet attempted to enter the harbor; but by this time Richelieu had equipped a number of large war vessels, and the English met with determined resistance. A storm damaged many of their vessels, and the battered fleet was forced to sail back to England. By this time one half of the population of La Rochelle had died. Of those left, few were strong enough to do military duty.

At length, after a siege of fifteen months, La Rochelle surrendered, and the king made a triumphal entry into the city. The fortifications were destroyed, and the power of the Huguenot nobles was forever at an end.

Richelieu compelled the nobles to admit that Louis was master of France. Many of them, however, were extremely angry at the loss of their power, and conspiracies against the life of Richelieu were more than once formed; but he always managed to find out about them and to punish those engaged in them. Many of the conspirators were executed; and thus Richelieu's power was actually increased instead of destroyed.

It should be said that though Richelieu destroyed the fortresses of the Huguenots, he was not unfair to them about their religion. They were allowed to worship God according to their own consciences. He was wise enough to know that people cannot be forced to worship in ways they do not like.

While Richelieu wished the king of France to be strong, he wished his neighbor, the emperor of Germany, to be weak. So in the same year in which he had broken down the power of the Protestant nobles of France, he actually gave help to the Protestant princes of Germany, who were fighting against the emperor just as the Huguenots had fought against King Louis.

He not only persuaded the great Gustavus Adolphus to lead his army of Swedes against the emperor, but he paid large sums of money to him for the support of his troops. Thus the great victories of Gustavus Adolphus, which were so valuable to the German Protestants, were won in part by soldiers paid and fed by Richelieu and the King of France.

Richelieu saw that if the emperor of Germany should overcome the Protestant princes and make himself head of the whole country, Germany would be a more powerful country than France. Then Germany might seek to conquer some of the territory of France. Richelieu fought the Protestants in France to make France united and strong. He paid and fed the Protestant armies in Germany to keep Germany divided and weak.

While Richelieu was prime minister of France, the English and Dutch were planting colonies in America; and commerce in the fish and furs which were brought from the New World was becoming very active and profitable.

Richelieu desired France to be the equal of England as a colonizing and commercial nation. He therefore gave a charter to the Company of "New France," as Canada was often called. He granted to the Company the sole right to collect furs in America, and the sole right to sell them in France. In return, the Company was required within fifteen years to land at least four thousand colonists in Canada.

To protect trading vessels from pirates who then infested the seas, to defend the coast of France, and to protect her colonies, Richelieu saw that a navy was required. He created the navy of France. When Louis XIII came to the throne the country had not a single war ship. When he died, the French navy consisted of twenty men-of-war and eighty smaller vessels.

Long before Richelieu died he had accomplished the object of his life. He had made the king of France an absolute monarch, and himself as absolute as the king.

Wallenstein had desired to accomplish the same thing in Germany, but he had miserably failed. Charles I was trying to make his power absolute in England, but the English people rebelled against him.

Many years after the death of Richelieu, the Czar, Peter the Great, visited Paris. As he stood before the splendid marble monument of Richelieu, he exclaimed, "Thou great man! I would have given thee one half of my dominions to learn from thee how to govern the other half."

King Charles I

Born in 1600, King of England from 1625 – 1649

Charles was born in Scotland on the 19th of November, 1600. He was the third child and second son of King James of Scotland and Anne of Denmark. When Elizabeth of England died in 1603, Charles' mother and father became King & Queen of England. They left almost immediately for London, along with his elder brother Henry, and his older sister Elizabeth. Charles' parents did not believe he was healthy enough to make the long overland journey, and so he was left behind in Scotland. A year later, he re-joined his family at the palace in the London.

When Charles was 12, his older brother Henry died of typhoid and he unexpectedly became the heir to the throne. When he was 13, his older sister Elizabeth married a German prince, Frederick V, Elector of the Palatinate and went to live with him at his court in Heidelberg.

After 1613, Charles grew up as the heir to the throne and was the only royal child at the court. In his teens, he formed a friendship with George Villiers, the Duke of Buckingham, who was his father's favorite. The story of their adventures in attempting to woo the Spanish princess has been told in the biography of King James. When the Spanish named their conditions for a wedding of their Princess Maria to Prince Charles, he found their terms insulting. So did Buckingham, so did King James I, and so did Parliament. The Spanish insisted that Charles must convert to Roman Catholicism, promise to raise any children as Roman Catholics, extend legal recognition to Catholics in England and grant them the right to worship in their own churches. Further Charles must have Parliament revise the laws so that Catholics could serve in the English government, and promise to remain in Spain for a year after the wedding. The terms were completely unacceptable to Charles and to everyone in England. Doubtless the Spanish knew this when they proposed them. Charles returned to England while Buckingham went to Paris to see if the French might be more agreeable to the marriage of the English prince to a French princess. They were. Cardinal Richelieu was happy to negotiate with Buckingham. Newly installed as Louis XIII's Secretary of State, Richelieu saw the advantages to France of an alliance with the English – especially if it had the effect of checking Spanish ambitions.

In the March of 1525, King James died. Prince Charles, 25 years old, became King Charles I. In May, Charles Stuart and Henrietta Maria were married by proxy and in June, in person. Parliament in England was uneasy. Many of their reasons for opposing the Spanish match applied equally to this new alliance with the French. And were not the French persecuting the Protestant Huguenots? Shouldn't the English come to the aid of fellow Protestants? What were the details of the arrangements made by Buckingham and Richelieu? Would Henrietta Maria raise the children of Charles as Protestants? Parliament insisted on answers. Charles bristled at being questioned.

Charles and Buckingham attempted to turn Parliament's anger towards Spain. They succeeded in persuading Parliament to grant revenues for the support of a war with Spain, but Parliament insisted that the grant of taxes would be for only a limited time. Charles was insulted and considered Parliament to have over-reached itself. Buckingham took matters in hand and organized a series of expeditions intended to challenge Spain and rescue Charles' sister Elizabeth and brother-in-law Frederick from their exile in the Netherlands and restore them to their palace in Heidelberg. Everything went badly. The German prince-general hired to re-conquer the Palatinate for Elizabeth and Frederick failed, and disbanded his troops. Buckingham organized a large naval expedition hoping to repeat Drake's raid on the Spanish port of Cadiz. The troops managed to land on the Spanish coast, but were forced into an embarrassing retreat when confronted by the superior numbers of the Spanish army. Buckingham sought the aid of Cardinal Richelieu on behalf of Frederick in regaining the Palatinate. Richelieu professed himself willing to help, but asked first for the assistance of English warships in laying siege to Huguenot rebels who had occupied an island off the coast of La Rochelle. Buckingham and Charles agreed, and again Parliament was outraged.

Two years later, circumstances had changed. The French had provided no assistance to Frederick and Elizabeth. Worse, they had refused to pay the second half of Henrietta Maria's dowry, and Charles desperately needed money. Charles and Buckingham now had a change of heart (or seemed to). They resolved to commit English forces to go to the aid of the Huguenots in La Rochelle, and summoned Parliament to request funds. Reluctantly, Parliament agreed. The expedition, led in person by Buckingham, went badly. Four thousand of the seven thousand English soldiers and sailors were killed. Buckingham was blamed for the failure. In the late summer of 1628, as he was preparing a second expedition to assist the Huguenots in La Rochelle, the Duke of Buckingham was stabbed and killed by a disgruntled army officer.

King Charles was distressed by the death of his friend. Buckingham was given a state funeral and buried in the great church at Westminster Abbey. The following spring, Charles approached Parliament for additional funds to pursue war against both France and Spain. When members of Parliament introduced resolutions of protest against Charles' collection of taxes without Parliament's authorization, Charles dissolved Parliament and resolved to rule without calling them again. He negotiated peace with both France and Spain, and successfully persuaded the French to pay the balance of his wife's dowry.

For several years, Charles was able to govern England without needing any grants or taxes from Parliament. In 1634, Charles issued a writ to all the counties of England re-imposing a tax from the days of King Edward I (1239-1307) known as "ship-money." Ship-money had been enacted to provide for the needs of the English navy and to insure that the costs were not unfairly borne solely by the ports. "Ship money" writs were dispatched by the King again in 1635, and again in 1636. It was clear that Charles had no intention of summoning Parliament again. By 1636, there was resistance in some parts of England to paying ship-money. One English nobleman brought a suit, asking the judges to declare the tax illegal. He lost the case, but 5 of the 12 judges voted against the king.

In 1630, Henrietta Maria gave birth to a son who was named Charles, after his father. In 1631, Mary was born. In 1633, James was born; in 1635, Elizabeth; and in 1637, Anne. Charles and Henrietta Maria now had five children, two sons and three daughters.

After the death of Buckingham, King Charles had two key advisors who assisted him during the 1630s in ruling England. The first was Thomas Wentworth, also known as Lord Strafford. Wentworth served in the King's council from 1628 on, and in 1632 King Charles made him Lord Deputy for Ireland. Ireland had been conquered by the English, but never subdued. The English government under Wentworth confiscated Irish land and gave it to English colonists and did its best to suppress the Catholic religion. Wentworth's harsh methods proved successful, at least in the short run.

William Laud,
Archbishop of Canterbury

Charles' second key advisor was the Archbishop of Canterbury, William Laud. Laud had long been a friend of both Buckingham and Charles. He had first been appointed a bishop by King James, who approved of his insistence that all priests in the Church of England should conform to the Anglican practices as prescribed in the prayer book. Laud disapproved of Puritans, dissenters, and non-conformists. In 1628, Charles appointed him as Bishop of London. In 1633, when the Archbishop of Canterbury died, Charles appointed Laud to succeed him. Laud, with the King's support, embarked on a campaign to impose uniformity on the church in both England and in Scotland. In England, Laud's policies increasingly embittered the Puritans who charged that Laud and Charles were secretly conspiring to return the Church of England to the fold of the Roman Catholic Church. In Scotland, feelings ran even higher. In 1637, Laud (with Charles' approval) moved to impose a new prayer book throughout the Church of Scotland. The Scottish clergy resisted. The Scottish nobles also resisted, forming an alliance dedicated to resisting all attempts to undo the Reformation of the Scottish church. These Scottish noblemen drew up and signed a National Covenant in 1638 and took the name "covenanters." The Covenanters and the Scottish clergy called for a General Assembly of the Scottish Church in the fall of 1638 and expelled all of the bishops of Scotland (from the church and the country) and declared that the Scottish Church would henceforth be governed by Presbyteries, or church councils. King Charles demanded that the General Assembly withdraw its actions and resolutions. The Covenanters refused.

Charles, with the support of Laud and Strafford (summoned home from Ireland), assembled an army and marched north towards Scotland. When the army reached the border with Scotland in the spring of 1639, however, great difficulties arose. The King did not have enough money to pay the expenses of the army. He was unable to equip the army, let alone provide it with sufficient supplies to launch an attack on Scotland. As summer dragged on, all that Charles could accomplish was to negotiate a temporary peace with the Scottish nobles – a peace that left them in charge of the rule of Scotland and which reiterated the actions of the General Assembly of the Scottish

Thomas Wentworth,
Earl of Strafford

Church. Humiliated, Charles returned to London and called for the election of Parliament in the spring of 1640. It had been eleven years since a Parliament had been called. When Parliament met, they proved reluctant to grant Charles an immediate supply of funds for the war with the Scottish Covenanters. Charles attempted at first to negotiate with key leaders in Parliament, but as negotiations drug out, he lost his temper. Urged on by Laud and Strafford, Charles dissolved Parliament barely a month after it had assembled and vowed he would defeat the Scots with his own resources. There were rumors that he might have Strafford bring an army of Irish Catholics to subdue Scotland. The Covenanters struck first. They marched their army into England and occupied the town of Newcastle which cut off London from its most important source of coal. Charles was then further humiliated and enraged when Laud and Strafford bluntly told him that there would be no funds and no army unless he could persuade Parliament to approve new taxes. With no resources to launch an attack against the Covenanters, Charles was forced to sign a humiliating provisional treaty with them in which he agreed to pay the expenses of the Scottish army and allow them to continue their occupation of Newcastle until a final treaty could be negotiated and approved in London.

The King then issued a call for a second set of Parliamentary elections, with the new Parliament to assemble in November. When they had assembled, the new Parliament refused to consider voting any funds for the king until he first agreed to sign several acts which would prevent any attempts at "personal rule" in the future. The Triennial Act required the King to summon Parliament at least every three years – if he did not, Parliament could summon itself! Parliament further demanded the dismissal of both Strafford and Laud before it would consider voting any funds for the King. When Charles resisted, Parliament passed acts of attainder against both men, sentencing them both to death. The leaders of Parliament told the King there would be no funds unless he signed the death warrants for his two chief advisors. Strafford wrote Charles and urged him to sign the warrant for his death, in hopes that it would reconcile the King with Parliament. Charles did so reluctantly, and Strafford was executed in May of 1641.

Parliament now renewed its attempts to reign in the power of the king to rule without their consent. In November, 1641 Parliament passed a Grand Remonstrance which enumerated those acts of the King which parliament considered to be unlawful and abusive. The Irish chose this moment to rise in rebellion against English rule. Charles sent a request to Parliament for funds to supply an army to put down the rebellion in Ireland. Parliament began to consider legislation that would take control of the army away from the King. When rumors reached Charles that certain members of Parliament were considering impeaching Queen Henrietta Maria, he had had enough. In January of 1642 he led a company of armed soldiers into the House of Commons, with the intent of personally arresting five members of the House. These five, having been warned, had already fled before the King could arrive. Charles was left standing in the House, with his soldiers, looking around helplessly and appearing impotent.

The breach between King and Parliament now became an open conflict. The King left London for the north of England to raise an army. The Queen and the younger royal children returned to her native France to raise funds. Civil War began with the Battle of Naseby in October of 1642 and continued until the siege of Oxford in April of 1646. Oxford was the King's last reliable base of support. When it was threatened, he slipped out of the city in disguise and fled north, and surrendered to the Scottish army at Newark. The Scots turned him over to the English Parliamentary army. The King was taken under arrest back to London and installed at Hampton Court, under a lenient house arrest. In November of 1647, Charles learned of rumors that some were plotting to kill him, and others to place him in the Tower of London. He fled from his house arrest at Hampton Court and made his way to the Isle of Wight, where he mistakenly believed that the governor was sympathetic. He would have done better to have crossed the channel to France. Instead, he was arrested again, and brought back to London. During the winter of 1647-1648 Charles corresponded with sympathizers and allies throughout England, and with the nobles leading the Scottish Army, which still occupied the north of England. In the spring of 1648 a rebellion against Parliament broke out and the Scottish army advanced south in support. The rebels cry was "We want to see our king!" The Parliamentary army had no trouble putting down this rebellion, which was over in a matter of days.

The officers of the Parliamentary army were outraged that Charles had continued to plot and deceive. They were furious that many of the remaining members in Parliament had appeared willing to plot with the King. Officers of the army sent soldiers to the House of Commons under the command of Colonel Pride to purge the House of royalist sympathizers. 45 MPs were arrested. 146 were turned away and told that they had been removed from Parliament. The Remaining 75 were allowed to continue to sit, and became known as the "Rump Parliament." The Rump Parliament consisted only of those who were opposed to the King and supporters of the army, which had now become an independent political power, under the command of its two chief officers, Fairfax and Cromwell.

The Rump Parliament passed an act establishing the High Court of Justice with 3 justices and 150 commissioners and proceeded to try King Charles I for high treason in the name of the people of England. The trial lasted for three weeks in January of 1649. The King challenged the authority of the court to try him. He asked "*I would know by what power I am called hither. I would know by what authority, I mean lawful authority.*" On January 27, 1649 the King was found guilty and sentenced to death. Fifty-nine commissioners signed the death warrant. Charles was executed three days later on January 30. His body was taken to Windsor castle, west of London (in a hearse drawn by six horses through the midst of a snowstorm), where he was buried in the royal vault alongside King Henry VIII and Queen Jane Seymour.

A View of the Place and Manner of K. Charles the Firsts Execution.

Charles was survived by three sons, Charles, James, and Henry who at his death were 19, 15, and 9 years old; and three daughters, Mary, Elizabeth, and Henrietta Anne, who at his death were 18, 14, and 5 years old. Both Elizabeth and Henry had remained behind in England. The rest of his children had gone into exile with Queen Henrietta Maria. Elizabeth and Henry were allowed to visit with their father for a few minutes before his execution. After his death, Henrietta Maria lived in France for many years, but returned to England in 1660 when their eldest son, Charles was restored to the throne as King Charles II. She spent the last four years of her life living in a convent she founded at Chaillot, a suburb of Paris. She is buried in the royal tombs at St. Denis.

Oliver Cromwell

1599–1658

Oliver Cromwell was born in Huntingdon, England, four years before the death of Queen Elizabeth and the accession of King James I.

His father was a gentleman farmer and cultivated his own land. But he was in comfortable circumstances and able to take excellent care of his family.

Oliver is described as being of a wayward and violent temper as a lad. He was cross and masterful; but possessed a large quantity of mirthful energy which showed itself in various forms of mischief.

It is said that when only a boy he dreamed that he would become the greatest man in England. A story is also told that once, at school, he took the part of king in a play, and placed the crown upon his head himself instead of letting someone else crown him.

At college he excelled in Latin and history, especially in the study of the lives of the famous men of Greece and Rome. He was, however, more famed for his skill at football and other rough games than for the study of books. His schooling was given him by Dr. Thomas Beard, a Puritan minister who resided in his native town, and who seems to have taken a great interest in him as a boy.

It was from his mother, who is described as "a woman of rare vigor and great decision of purpose," that Cromwell derived his remarkable strength of character.

At the age of eighteen he left college, on account of the death of his father, and returned home to look after the affairs of the family. At twenty-one years of age he was married to Elizabeth Bourchier, daughter of a London merchant, who proved to be a most excellent wife.

The esteem in which he was held in Huntingdon is shown by the fact that in the Great Parliament of 1628, which drew up "The Petition of Rights," he sat as a member and represented his native place. He made his first speech in the House of Commons, where so much of his future work was to be done, on February 11, 1629. He was then thirty years of age.

A gentleman who heard this first speech has thus described it: "I came into the House of Commons one morning and listened to a gentleman speaking whom I knew not. His dress was a plain cloth suit which showed the cut of a country tailor; his linen was not very clean; his hat was without a hatband; his voice was sharp, and his eloquence full of fervor. He was speaking in behalf of a servant who had been imprisoned for speaking against the queen because she indulged in dancing."

After King Charles dismissed that Parliament, he decided to manage the affairs of the nation without one; and so for eleven years no other Parliament was called.

During this long interval Cromwell remained at home and worked upon his land.

War with the Scottish nobles, and want of money at last forced King Charles to call a Parliament; and it assembled in 1640. In this Parliament Cromwell sat as the member for Cambridge, and took an active part in the business of the House.

Trouble soon arose between the king and the Parliament on the question as to who possessed the right to levy taxes. Both parties claimed this right and neither would yield. Then Parliament passed what was called "The Great Remonstrance," which was a complaint from the people of the wrongs they suffered under the rule of Charles.

On leaving the house that day, Cromwell said to a friend with whom he was walking, "If the Remonstrance had been rejected I would have left England never to have set my foot upon her shores again."

The king was so angry that he ordered the arrest of the five members who had taken the lead in the passing of the Remonstrance; but the House of Commons would not allow the arrests to be made. The next day King Charles brought four hundred soldiers with him, and demanded that the men be given up; but the members would not yield, and the king had to go away without them.

It became evident that there would be war between the Parliament and the king, and the whole land was filled with excitement and alarm. How Cromwell felt about this matter can be seen from a few words in a letter written at this time. He said, "The king's heart has been hardened. He will not listen to reason. The sword must be drawn. I feel myself urged to carry forward this work."

The whole nation quickly became divided into two parties. The friends of the king were called "Royalists," or "Cavaliers." Those of Parliament were called "Roundheads." Cromwell's own uncle and cousin were staunch friends of King Charles, and at once entered his army.

Cromwell raised two companies of volunteers. He distinguished himself by his strict discipline, although up to the time when the war broke out he had not had much experience in military affairs. He was then forty-three years old. He soon became known as a great leader and soldier; and his successes as a soldier gave him a high place in the affairs of the nation.

The adherents of Parliament had on their side the navy; and they also had more money than King Charles had. But Charles had a fine body of cavalry; and many of the rich men of England sent him money to carry on the war.

At the opening of the war the army of Charles had the advantage. Cromwell saw that the forces of the Parliament would soon be beaten unless they could get soldiers who were interested in the cause for which they were fighting; and such men he at once began to gather about him. A large number of soldiers who fought under Cromwell were Puritans. The Puritans were people who objected to many of the forms and ceremonies of the Church of England.

Many of them laid great stress on the importance of sober and righteous living. When in camp, they read the Bible and sang psalms. They often recited Bible verses and sang psalms as they went into battle.

The first battle of the war was fought at Edge Hill. The greatest loss in any single engagement was at the battle of Marston Moor, where the king's army left forty thousand slain upon the field. In this battle the soldiers under the command of Cromwell really won the victory. From that time he rose rapidly until he became commander-in-chief of the army. He is said to have been victorious in every battle he fought.

While in the army, Oliver received the name of "Ironsides;" and a little later this same title was given to his men, because the Royalist troops had found it impossible to break Cromwell's lines.

But it must not be thought that Cromwell was a man devoid of tender feeling. Shortly before the battle of Marston Moor his eldest son was killed. Cromwell felt his loss most keenly, and was heard to say, "It went to my heart like a dagger. Indeed it did."

Over sixty other battles were fought; and finally the cause of the king was wrecked at the great battle of Naseby, in 1645.

But instead of admitting that he was beaten, and agreeing to meet the demands of the people, Charles fled to Scotland and tried to induce the Scots to give him aid.

This turned Cromwell against the king, and convinced him that only through the death of Charles was it possible to secure the liberties of the English people.

In June, 1647, the king was seized by one of Cromwell's soldiers and placed in custody of the army. The Commons resented this action and resolved to make terms with the king. Whereupon the army leaders sent Colonel Pride with a body of soldiers to "purge" the Commons of members who favored making terms with the king.

The remaining members soon afterwards passed a resolution that the king should be brought to justice, and voted to form a special High Court of Justice. The king protested that the court was illegal and refused to make any plea. He was condemned by the court and was beheaded on January 30, 1649.

In 1653 Cromwell decided to dissolve' Parliament. A body of soldiers drove the members out and Cromwell himself took possession of the speaker's mace. Oliver Cromwell was now the most powerful man in England; and the army, over which he still presided, offered to make him king. One of his daughters pleaded so earnestly with him that he refused to accept the crown or to take the title of king.

Cromwell dissolving the Rump Parliament

England was declared to be no longer a monarchy but a Commonwealth; and under this new form of government Oliver Cromwell was made ruler, with the title of Protector.

In the summer of 1658 he was taken ill with chills and fever; and on September 3rd of that year he died.

Oliver Cromwell had grave faults; and he was by no means an easy man to deal with. He made many blunders, some of which were serious ones. But no one ever challenged his personal integrity or did anything but wonder at the passion and energy with which he pursued the cause of godly government.

William Bradford

1590-1657

THE MAYFLOWER COMPACT · 1620

When William Bradford was born in 1590 in the midland English village of Austerfield, Queen Elizabeth was at the zenith of her popularity and influence. Bradford's family were sturdy farmers who owned land outside the village and raised sheep. They were independent, but not wealthy. They had no titles of nobility but they enjoyed the respect of the other families of the village. Bradford, as the eldest son, was destined to inherit all of the property. Bradford's father died before he was two years old. Two years later, young William's mother re-married. William was sent to live with his grandfather. When he was six, his grandfather died. William returned to live with his mother and step-father, but his mother died a year later, and he then went to live with his uncles. At seven years old, William had lived in four households. All those closest to him had died. He was an orphan. We know two things about Bradford's education – he learned to read and write, but he was not enrolled in any local school. From his later writings, we can discern that he read the books which were most widely distributed in his day: **The Bible**, Foxe's **Book of Martyrs**, and Erasmus' **Praise of Folly**. These books would have been the mainstay of many a local clergyman's library – and it is by one of these that Bradford likely was taught.

At a young age, Bradford began to think independently in matters of religion. Opinion in the parishes of England was divided between those who were satisfied with maintaining the unity and conformity of the Church of England, and those who believed that the church was in need of further reform. When he was twelve, Bradford stopped attending the local parish church in Austerfield. Instead, he began rising early on each Sunday morning and walking eight miles to attend services at the congregation in Babworth where the priest, Richard Clyfton, preached that the Church of England was in desperate need of reform. Young William's uncles were embarrassed and displeased with their nephew's scandalous activity. They warned him, scolded him, and threatened him, trying to make him cease going to services in Bradford. They pleaded with him that he was jeopardizing all their reputations. They feared that Clyfton's preaching would sooner or later come to the attention of church authorities and everyone in the congregation would be punished. Month after month, young William persisted, rising early and walking the eight miles to Babworth for services and preaching and then making the long eight-mile walk home.

Soon after he began attending services at Babworth, young William Bradford was befriended by one of the elders of the congregation. William Brewster was a prominent landowner who lived, conveniently for William, on the road from Austerfield and Babworth. Partway to church, Bradford could join his older friend, Mr. William Brewster and together they would walk the remaining miles. Brewster was the resident steward (or manager) for a small estate owned by the Archbishop of York on the road between Austerfield and Babworth called Scrooby Manor. William Brewster's father had been manager of the estate before him, and there was every expectation that his eldest son would continue to hold the post when Brewster retired. Brewster himself had received an education at Cambridge and spent time in London at the court of Queen Elizabeth. He had served as secretary to William Davidson, who was assistant Secretary of State to Elizabeth. When Elizabeth had finally been persuaded to sign the death warrant for the execution of her cousin Mary, Queen of Scots, it was Davidson who handled the paperwork. Afterwards, Elizabeth regretted her decision and blamed Davidson. She threw him into prison in the Tower and confiscated his estates. Brewster had remained loyal to Davidson. When Davidson was finally freed from prison and (partially) forgiven by Elizabeth, he retired from the court to his estate. Brewster returned to Scrooby Manor.

William Brewster had seen much more of the world than anyone else living in Babworth or Austerfield. He had been to University at Cambridge. He had traveled to the Netherlands with

Davidson to negotiate a treaty with the Dutch. It was natural that he should play a leading role in the little congregation at Babworth. In 1603, Bradford was 13, and his friend Brewster was 37, with two young children (Jonathan 10, and Patience 3) of his own.

In 1603, Queen Elizabeth died and King James of Scotland became King of England. Richard Clyfton, Elder William Brewster, and the congregation at Babworth had high hopes that the new King might heed the calls for reform and be God's instrument to complete the reformation of the English church. They were bitterly disappointed. King James, as you have read, vowed to make the Puritans conform to the Church of England, or else to "harry them out of the land." Clyfton resigned his post as Parish priest in Babworth. Pastor Clifton and Elder Brewster agreed that the Church of England was not likely to be reformed in King James' lifetime. They then took the dramatic step to separate themselves from the Church of England. It was a dramatic step because it was illegal. There were no "alternative" churches in any town, village, or city of England to choose from. The principle all over Europe was *cuius regio, eius religio* (his region, his religion) – all of the subjects of a king or prince were compelled, by force of law, to adopt his religion. Clyfton and Brewster had taken the dangerous and unprecedented step of becoming non-conformists - Separatists. Sixteen-year-old William Bradford became a Separatist along with them. Most of the congregation from Babworth joined them, and the church of about 40 souls, began to meet discreetly, if not completely secretly, at the estate managed by William Brewster, Scrooby Manor.

For several years they managed to avoid any trouble with any of the authorities, but it was doubtful they would avoid notice forever. Austerfield was a small town of perhaps 150. Every Sunday, 40-50 people arrived at Scrooby Manor and stayed all day. In 1607, five members of the Scrooby Separatist congregation, (including the 40 year old William Brewster, but not the 17 year old Bradford), were summoned to the Church court of the Archbishop of York, and were found guilty of being "disobedient in matters of religion." They were each fined, and ordered to return to their parish churches and to cease meeting separately and conducting unauthorized and illegal religious services.

Obedience to this order was not something the Separatists could, in good conscience, do. They resolved to leave England and emigrate to a foreign country where they would be free to continue their religious services in the manner they saw fit. It was a momentous and dangerous decision. Emigration itself would be a further offense. Brewster and Clyfton advised the congregation, most of whom had never traveled beyond the English county in which they had been born, to sell all of their possessions and to prepare to leave the country for the Netherlands.

The first attempt to leave England ended in frightening failure. The ship captain they hired to meet them along the eastern coast of England took their money and then betrayed them to the authorities. They were arrested and held in a local jail for a month. Then charges against them were dismissed and they were told to go home. But they no longer had homes to go to. In the spring of 1608, they tried to leave England again, this time by hiring a Dutch captain. He was faithful to his bargain, but when the group was surprised while ferrying passengers from the shore, he refused to risk having his ship seized and sailed off, leaving half the congregation (mostly women and children) behind. Clyfton, Brewster, and Bradford chose to voluntarily stay behind to protect them. Somehow, they were able to arrange for families to take passage across the North Sea in small groups and be reunited in the Netherlands. By the summer of 1608 all of the Scrooby Separatists were in Amsterdam. It would be hard to imagine a city more different from the village of Austerfield. Amsterdam was a crowded, bustling, port city with a population of over 200,000. It was criss-crossed by narrow cobblestoned alleys and brackish canals. Relatively quickly, the group of English families decided Amsterdam was not for them. By the end of the year, they had moved to Leyden, a smaller, quieter city 25 miles to the southwest. Pastor Richard Clyfton decided to remain in Amsterdam. His assistant, John Robinson, moved to Leyden with the little congregation and became their pastor.

After two years in Leyden, the Scrooby Separatists were able to purchase a large house for the congregation to meet in, and where their minister could live. From 1609-1612, Bradford lived with the Brewster family. In 1612, 22-year-old William Bradford became a citizen of the city of Leyden and became a member of the weaver's guild. A year before, he had come into his inheritance from his father. He arranged for the land and house in Austerfield to be sold, and he used the proceeds to purchase a house and set up a workshop for himself in Leyden. At the end of the year, he married Dorothy May, a member of the English Separatist group in Amsterdam. Bradford now had a home of his own, a trade, and was a promising young member of the English Separatist Church in Leyden. In 1614, a son, whom they named John, was born to William and Dorothy. But within four years, the members of the church had decided that they must leave Leyden. There were several reasons for this. Their children were increasingly influenced by Dutch culture. They were learning the Dutch language – some knew it better than their parents' English – and were adopting Dutch ways. The Dutch did not observe the Sabbath nearly as strictly as the Separatists, and their children tended to adopt the Dutch outlook and attitude about such things. There continued to be threats of persecution. Not from the Dutch, but from the English and the Spanish. The Spanish had not yet surrendered their claim to rule the Netherlands, and threatened to renew their military campaign to re-assert control. King James in England disliked all religious dissenters and from time to time the English ambassador urged the city councilors in Leyden to expel the English Separatists, who were, he said, fugitives from English justice. The Separatists, led by Pastor Robinson and Elder Brewster decided they must leave Leyden. They read Captain John Smith's glowing account of his voyage exploring the coast of New England, but eventually decided to sail to Virginia and establish their own settlement near Jamestown. They sent two leaders of the congregation (Robert Cushman and John Carver) to London to negotiate with the Virginia Company. The negotiations took two years. There were many details to work out, and the Separatists sought assurances that they would be allowed to continue their reformed religious services and not be compelled to rejoin the Church of England. When they had finally reached agreement on a patent (a grant of land from the King) for their new settlement in Virginia, new complications arose. The Virginia Company had no money left to purchase supplies or charter a ship to take them to North America. In the early spring of 1620, representatives of the New Netherlands Company went to

Leyden with a proposal. They offered both transportation and supplies if the congregation would settle in the Dutch colony at the mouth of the Hudson River. As the Separatists were pondering this offer, they received yet another proposal. Thomas Weston, representing a group of London merchants arrived and offered to invest in ships and supplies in exchange for a promise to be repaid from the earnings of the colonists once they were established. Although not happy with all of the financial details, the Separatists agreed to Weston's proposal. Those who would go to establish the colony began to sell their land & houses in Leyden and to prepare for the voyage. They hoped to sail quickly – in a matter of just a few weeks – in order to reach North America in time to grow and harvest at least some crops before the onset of winter. It was decided that Pastor Robinson should remain behind to help those families who would come in the second or third year. Elder Brewster (and deacons Carver and Cushman) would go with the first group of colonists. William Bradford (now 30 years old) and his wife Dorothy would go with the initial group. Their young son John (who was only 6) would be cared for in Leyden by another family and would join his parents later. It took longer to sell property, collect supplies, and charter ships than anyone had imagined. May passed into June which turned into July. On July 21st a little party of fifty Pilgrims set out from Leyden. A few days later, they reached Southampton where they were joined by another fifty colonists who had been recruited by Weston and the London merchants. Twice they set out to the west and twice had to turn back when one of their two ships began leaking. Finally, after transferring everyone to the one sound ship, the Mayflower, they set off on September 6th from the port of Plymouth.

Champlain had been making the Atlantic crossing for twenty years when the Pilgrims set sail. Its duration varied from 30 to 70 days. For the Pilgrims, it took 66 days. On November 10, 1620, they spotted the sandy beaches of Cape Cod on the horizon. It was much too late for any crops to be grown. They would have to hurry to find a suitable site for their settlement and prepare for the winter. Two events during the long voyage made a deep impression on Bradford. One of the young sailors took great delight in insulting and cursing the Pilgrims and predicting their imminent demise and deaths in the terrible forests of the New World. About four weeks into the voyage, the young sailor suddenly took ill and died.

And then, halfway across the Atlantic the Mayflower was caught for days in a powerful storm. One of the young men, John Howland, about twenty years old, went up on deck during the storm and was washed overboard. Providentially, he managed to grab one of the ropes trailing from the Mayflower's sails and hold on until he could be hauled back on board. Fifty-three years later, he would die as the last surviving Mayflower passenger.

Although they had reached land, the coast of Cape Cod was unsuitable for a colony. It was a narrow, sandy peninsula with poor sources of fresh water. The Pilgrims prepared to launch a small boat, called a shallop, so that they could explore the coast. But before they set off, all 41 of the men signed a short pledge or agreement:

> In the name of God, Amen. We whose names are underwritten, the loyal subjects of our dread Sovereign Lord King James, by the Grace of God of Great Britain, France and Ireland, King, Defender of the Faith, etc.
>
> Having undertaken, for the Glory of God and advancement of the Christian Faith and Honour of our King and Country, a Voyage to plant the First Colony in the Northern Parts of Virginia, do by these presents solemnly and mutually in the presence of God and one of another, Covenant and Combine ourselves together into a Civil Body Politic, for our better ordering and preservation and furtherance of the ends aforesaid; and by virtue hereof to enact, constitute and frame such just and equal Laws, Ordinances, Acts, Constitutions and Offices, from time to time, as shall be thought most meet and convenient for the general good of the Colony, unto which we promise all due submission and obedience. In witness whereof we have hereunder subscribed our names at Cape Cod, the 11th of November, in the year of the reign of our Sovereign Lord King James, of England, France and Ireland the eighteenth, and of Scotland the fifty-fourth. Anno Domini 1620.

This short document is called the Mayflower Compact. It bound all of the passengers, Pilgrims from Leyden and Strangers from London, into one "body politic," with a pledge from each to obey the laws of the colony. The 41 signers then elected Deacon John Carver as Governor of their colony. The following day was the Sabbath, and the Pilgrims would do no work or exploration. They held religious services and spent the day in prayer, scripture reading, and meditation. On Monday, a small group of about 16 men (including Bradford) under the command of Captain Miles Standish (the Pilgrim's military advisor) began their exploration of the coast. On December 11th, with winter already making its presence felt, they found what they were looking for – across the bay from Cape Cod was a protected harbor, with hills, woods, streams, and rich soil. The men in the exploring party returned to the Mayflower in order to direct everyone to the spot. It was then that William Bradford learned that his wife Dorothy had drowned while he had been exploring the coast.

William, 30 years old was now a widower. His son had lost his mother at the same age he had.

On December 25th, with the Mayflower at anchor in the harbor, all of the Pilgrims went on shore and were busy with the tasks of building a permanent settlement. Christmas Day was not a holiday that they celebrated, finding no warrant for it in the Scriptures. The Pilgrims laid out a single street from the shore directly up a prominent hill. On both sides of the street, they built 19 houses, each about twenty feet by twenty feet, for the 19 families. In January, people started dying. More settlers died in February. By March, 50 of the 101 Pilgrims were dead. The sailors on board the Mayflower, anchored in the harbor, were not spared either. Half of them died. Brewster and Standish were among the few who did not fall ill. At times there were only five or six people well enough to care for the sick. Bradford (sick himself for several weeks) wrote later that they did their work as nurses cheerfully, without complaining.

Although they had seen Indians, off and on, from a distance, as yet they had had no contact with them. In March, that changed. An Indian walked into the settlement and began speaking to the Pilgrims – in English! His name was Samoset and he had learned English from the crews of English fishing boats which had been frequenting the coast further to the north. He explained to the Pilgrims that the land where they had settled formerly belonged to the Pawtuxet tribe, but that all of the members of the tribe had mysteriously died a few years before. The neighboring tribes had not settled on their land for fear of catching the same disease. They were not alarmed by the Pilgrim's arrival, but viewed them as simply a replacement tribe for the Pawtuxets – albeit with funny clothes, hats, and strange dwellings.

Several days later, Samoset returned with the chief of his tribe, Massasoit, and 60 warriors – three times as many men as the surviving Pilgrims could muster. Along with them was another Indian who spoke English, Squanto. Squanto was the only surviving member of the Pawtuxet tribe. He had been living with Samoset's tribe, but now agreed to settle with the Pilgrims.

Spring came slowly in New England. The days got a bit less chilly and there were a few minutes more sunlight each day. Gradually, the surviving Pilgrims regained their strength. In April the Mayflower sailed out of the harbor, headed home for England. Shortly after the sailing of the Mayflower, Governor Carver collapsed and died. After he was buried, the Pilgrims elected William Bradford, age 32, as their new Governor. Over the next 36 years, he would be elected Governor 30 times. Assisting and advising Bradford would be elder William Brewster, then aged 55, Captain Miles Standish, aged 34 and Edward Winslow, age 26. Squanto lived with Governor Bradford all through the spring and summer of 1621 and spent his time patiently teaching the Pilgrims about how the Indians grew crops, using fish to fertilize corn, how to catch eels and fish, and advised them on their dealings with the surrounding Indian tribes.

In the fall the Pilgrims were able to harvest the crops they had planted and by following Squanto's advice they had an abundance of food. Governor Bradford called for a general day of Thanksgiving to God for the good harvest. Through Squanto, he invited Chief Massasoit and the entire Wampanoag tribe to join them. And thus 50 Pilgrims and 90 Indians sat down together at trestle tables for the first Thanksgiving Feast in 1621.

A month later a supply ship, the *Fortune*, arrived from England with tools, seed, and 35 more colonists from the Separatist congregation back in Leyden. When the ship returned to England later in the month, it took with it an encouraging account of the colony written by

Bradford and Edward Winslow, which would be published in London with the title, "**Mourt's Relation.**" Bradford also took care to see to it that the ship was filled with furs and other goods from the new world which could be sold to help pay the colonists' debt to the London merchants who had invested in the colony.

In 1622, the Pilgrim colony at Plymouth suffered a great loss when Squanto, their Indian guide fell ill and died.

The London merchants had so far, had little return for their investment. They now sent several shiploads of men, not to re-supply the Pilgrims, but to establish additional outposts in the hopes that one or more of them might prove an economic success. But without the strong family ties which bound the Pilgrims of Plymouth together, these other outposts failed. None of them lasted more than a year, though the Pilgrims often shared their limited supplies with them.

More colonists for Plymouth arrived each year. In 1623, Bradford married one of the new colonists, Alice Carpenter Southworth, and became stepfather to her two children. William and Alice would eventually have four children of their own. In 1627, Bradford's son from his first marriage, John, now 13 years old, re-joined his father in the New World. The Bradfords also took in several children from other Pilgrim families where one or both parents had died. Bradford took seriously his obligation to educate his children and spent part of each day teaching the children of the household their lessons.

Plymouth now had a population of about 180. It would never grow much larger. As more colonists arrived, older established families moved out and established farmsteads in the surrounding countryside. Cattle were brought over from England and raised for milk and meat, as well as being hitched to plows to bring more land under cultivation. In 1630, the last immigrants from Leyden arrived. John Robinson, their pastor in Leyden was never able to join his flock in their new colony. He died in Ledyen in 1625.

In 1629 another small group of religious settlers arrived and established a settlement north of Plymouth. These were Puritans. They fervently wished for reform of the Church of England and, unlike the Pilgrims, they had not become Separatists. In the summer of 1630, a fleet of eleven ships brought over seven hundred Puritans to join their colony. It also brought a new governor for the Puritans, John Winthrop. Like the Pilgrims they faced terrible conditions in their first few years. They appealed to the Pilgrims in Plymouth for help, and Governor Bradford sent them their physician. Bradford's charity, friendship, and assistance did much to foster peaceful relations between the two neighboring settlements.

One year after the settlement was established at Boston, in November of 1631, William Bradford took one of Plymouth colony's boats and a handful of his assistants and sailed north from Plymouth Harbor to Boston Harbor. There he met with Governor Winthrop of the Massachusetts Bay colony and celebrated a day of Thanksgiving with him and his Puritan settlers.

From 1630 to 1640 a further 20,000 Puritans emigrated from England to the Massachusetts Bay Colony which quickly became much larger than Plymouth. The population of Plymouth colony and all of its outlying farmsteads never exceeded 3,000 people. In 1691 King William in England reorganized the charters for the various settlements in New England, and Plymouth was absorbed into the Province of Massachusetts Bay.

Through the 1630s, and 1640s, Bradford continued to be elected Governor of the Plymouth colony. Over the 37 years from 1621 to 1657, he was elected governor 30 times. His only times out of office were when he declined to run, protesting that he must have some relief and a year of rest. Elder William Brewster died in 1644. Governor John Winthrop had died in 1649. Miles Standish died in 1656.

In May of 1657, after a short illness, William Bradford died, and was buried at Plymouth. On his grave marker is carved the Latin epitaph: *"qua patres difficillime adepti sunt nolite turpiter relinquere*" "What our forefathers with so much difficulty secured, do not basely relinquish."

John Winthrop

1588-1649

John Winthrop was born in 1588, the year of the Spanish Armada, in Edwardstone, England. Edwardstone is in Suffolk County, near the eastern coast, in the Stour River valley. Winthrop came from a wealthy family. His father had been educated at Cambridge and was a lawyer who took cases both in Suffolk County and in London. The contrast between the social backgrounds of Winthrop and Bradford, the two parallel colonial governors in Massachusetts, could hardly have been greater. What they had in common was a deep commitment to Christ.

In the Stour valley, unlike the Yorkshire of Bradford and Brewster, those who wished to complete the reformation of the Church of England were in the majority, and were able to protect Puritan pastors from dismissal. In fact, the region of England where Winthrop grew up was celebrated and admired by Puritans throughout England as an example of a "godly community" where the unfettered gospel was preached in the parish churches and many of the symbols of the old Roman church had been discarded and were no longer used.

The Winthrops were a well known and established family in the region. They had no titles of nobility and were not the wealthiest, but their land holdings were significant. Following in his father's footsteps, John was admitted to Cambridge in 1602, at the age of 14. The following year, Elizabeth died and James became King.

In 1604, John traveled to East Anglia with one of his classmates from Cambridge. There he met, and fell in love with Mary Forth, his classmate's cousin. One year later, they married, and Winthrop left Cambridge.

For the first few years of their marriage, John and Mary lived with Mary's father, John Forth, on his estates in East Anglia. John and Mary had three sons, born in 1606, 1608, 1610, and a daughter born in 1612. In 1613, Mary's father died. John and Mary inherited all of his lands. Shortly thereafter they moved backed to Groton, and moved into Groton Manor, which John's father Adam had worked for several years to purchase from his brother (John's uncle). Adam Winthrop had for many years been a successful lawyer. He had married late and his children had been born while he was in his forties. He was now 65 and ready to retire from life in London and live out his days on his country estates in Suffolk. He and his wife Anne were pleased to welcome John and Mary and their four grandchildren and to see them settled in the family manor at Groton. John renewed his friendships in the Stour valley.

John Winthrop, a young father of 25, felt a very deep and renewed commitment to Christ. When he moved back to Groton Manor, he joined a small group of local clergy and interested laymen. They drew up and signed a covenant to encourage each other in their Christian faith. The group met weekly, on Fridays for prayer and Bible study and discussion of the sermons they had heard. At about the same time, John was admitted to Gray's Inn in London where he began to study law. In 1615, he was appointed to the Suffolk County Commission. This was the governing body that met quarterly, at the time of the circuit court sessions, and regulated the affairs of the county.

After moving to Groton, in June of 1614, Mary gave birth to their fifth child, a little girl whom they named Anne, but the baby died a week after her birth. The next year, in June of 1615, Mary Winthrop gave birth to their sixth child, also christened Anne. But both mother and child died two days later. John, at 28, was a widower, with four small children aged 9, 7, 5, and 3. Six months later, in December, John Winthrop married for a second time, to Thomasine

Clopton of Groton, whom he had known since his childhood. She was 33. In 1616, just before their first wedding anniversary, Thomasine gave birth to a daughter who died two days later. Thomasine came down with a high fever. She lingered for a week and died the day after their first anniversary. John was crushed with grief. He had been very close to both Mary and to Thomasine. He had shared a deep Christian faith with both of them, and his affectionate letters to them are evidence of his love.

But John was once again widowed, and once again concerned with how to care for his children, though his parents no doubt took over their charge whenever John traveled to London or to a quarter session of the county commission. In 1617, John met Margaret Tyndale, who lived a half a day's ride to the south of Groton Manor. He was now 29. Margaret was a few years younger. After a short courtship, they were married in April of 1618. In March of 1619, Margaret gave birth to a son, christened Stephen. When she fell ill with a fever, John began to fast and pray for her healing. Ten days later, a group of "godly ministers" met together to pray for Margaret Winthrop, and at the very hour they were praying, her fever broke and she recovered.

Margaret quickly became John's partner in the management of Groton Manor and the fields and property in the surrounding area. She and John rose early each day and had devotions with their children and with all of the household servants and farm laborers – a small congregation of perhaps 20-30 people! While John supervised work in the fields (when he was not in London studying the law or traveling in Suffolk to meetings of the County Commission), Margaret took charge of the household servants and the instruction of all five of their children.

In 1623, Winthrop's father Adam died at the age of 75. He had been retired from the practice of law for ten years and had turned the management of all of his lands and interests over to his son. A few years later, John's oldest son, John, Jr. (sometimes called John Winthrop the younger) was old enough to enter the Inns of Court in London and begin his own path to a career as a lawyer.

John's second son, Henry, was not a scholar. In 1627, at the age of 19, he sailed with an English expedition to the West Indies. He stayed in Barbados, and tried his luck at planting tobacco. The harvests were poor and he lost money and had to return to England in 1629. John's third son, Forth, felt a calling to become a minister. In 1626, he began his studies in theology at Cambridge.

At home in Groton, developments in both religion and politics troubled John Winthrop. The Puritan reforms in the Stour Valley had been slowly, but steadily, reversed or curtailed. Ministers who would not conform to the high church practices favored first by King James and then by King Charles found themselves harassed or dismissed from their offices. Charles in particular, seemed to get off on the wrong foot with both Parliament and Puritan ministers in the Church of England. The Puritans strongly disapproved of his marriage to a French Catholic princess. And they were alarmed by his stubborn attempts to raise taxes without the authorization of Parliament. His appointment of William Laud as bishop was particularly disheartening to the Puritans, as Laud began to remove ministers who would not conform to the prayer book and use the forms and symbols of "high church" Anglicanism.

John Winthrop became disillusioned about the prospects for reform of the church or redress of the political situation in England. When King Charles angrily dismissed the Parliament he had summoned in January of 1629, Winthrop began to think of emigration. He considered Ireland briefly, but he soon joined other Puritans who had been promoting the idea of a colony in New England. For several years, leading Puritans in Cambridge and other prominent eastern English towns had been organizing and recruiting investors and colonists for a Puritan settlement in New England. Across the Atlantic Ocean, they would be free to establish both religious and political life in the ways they believed Christianity demanded. By August of 1629, Winthrop had become one of the leaders of the movement. He spoke and wrote often of the sound reasons for leaving England and carrying the gospel to the New World.

In October, 1629 at a meeting of the Massachusetts Bay Company in Cambridge, Winthrop was chosen to be the governor of the company and the colony it would plant. Although not the largest investor in the new company, Winthrop had made clear his resolve to sell all of his lands in England and make a permanent move to the New World. He pledged the equivalent of several hundred thousand dollars as his investment. The other company shareholders and colonists evidently preferred Winthrop to other wealthier candidates, not least because he would be making the voyage with them. At its October meeting, the company also made the unprecedented decision to transfer the management and governance of the colony to New England with the colonists. The affairs of the company would not be managed by directors back in England. The directors would be colonists themselves and they would manage their own affairs from the site of the colony in the new world.

Once Winthrop was elected governor of the company, he faced the daunting task of chartering ships and securing supplies for the 700 colonists who had made the decision to emigrate. Where the Plymouth colonists had numbered only 100 and traveled in a single ship, the colonists of the Massachusetts Bay Company would cross in a fleet of eleven ships. Organizing the fleet was a huge task and took many months.

As winter passed into spring, all of the preparations were completed. Winthrop and the other Puritan colonists assembled in the English port of Southampton where their fleet of ships lay at anchor, loaded with stores for the voyage and the first year. In March of 1630, all seven hundred colonists and many of their English friends gathered in the Church of the Holy Rood to seek God's blessing on their efforts. After prayers and a sermon by the reverend John Cotton, Winthrop rose to address the assembly. He chose as his topic, "The Model of Christian Charity," and in his address he urged and exhorted the 700 colonists to be knit together in one body, bound to each other by Christ's love. He observed that while the parts of the body are different from each other, the body becomes perfect when the parts are joined together by love. He reminded them that, being knit together in a body, "If one member suffers, all suffer with it; if one be in honor, all rejoice with it." And he charged all of the colonists to care for each other in the difficult days ahead: He quoted 1 John 3:16, "We ought to lay down our lives for the brethren" and Gal. 6:2, "Bear ye one another's burden's and so fulfill the law of Christ."

Finally, in a stirring conclusion, Winthrop admonished the colonists that they must love and tenderly care for one another, for the eyes of the world would be upon them, watching to see what sort of success or failure those who professed to be building a Christian community might have:

> Now the only way to avoid this shipwreck, and to provide for our posterity, is to follow the counsel of Micah, to do justly, to love mercy, to walk humbly with our God. For this end, we must be knit together, in this work, as one man. We must entertain each other in brotherly affection. We must be willing to abridge ourselves of our superfluities, for the supply of others' necessities. We must uphold a familiar commerce together in all meekness, gentleness, patience and liberality. We must delight in each other; make others' conditions our own; rejoice together, mourn together, labor and suffer together, always having before our eyes our commission and community in the work, as members of the same body. So shall we keep the unity of the spirit in the bond of peace. The Lord will be our God, and delight to dwell among us, as His own people, and will command a blessing upon us in all our ways, so that we shall see much more of His wisdom, power, goodness and truth, than formerly we have been acquainted with. We shall find that the God of Israel is among us, when ten of us shall be able to resist a thousand of our enemies; when He shall make us a praise and glory that men shall say of succeeding plantations, "may the Lord make it like that of New England." **For we must consider that we shall be as a city upon a hill. The eyes of all people are upon us. So that if we shall deal falsely with our God in this work we have undertaken, and so cause Him to withdraw His present help from us, we shall be made a story and a by-word through the world.** We shall open the mouths of enemies to speak evil of the ways of God, and all professors for God's sake. We shall shame the faces of many of God's worthy servants, and cause their prayers to be turned into curses upon us till we be consumed out of the good land whither we are going.

> And to shut this discourse with that exhortation of Moses, that faithful servant of the Lord, in his last farewell to Israel, Deut. 30. "Beloved, there is now set before us life and death, good and evil," in that we are commanded this day to love the Lord our God, and to love one another, to walk in his ways and to keep his Commandments and his ordinance and his laws, and the articles of our Covenant with Him, that we may live and be multiplied, and that the Lord our God may bless us in the land whither we go to possess it. **But if our hearts shall turn away, so that we will not obey, but shall be seduced, and worship other Gods, our pleasure and profits, and serve them; it is**

propounded unto us this day, we shall surely perish out of the good land whither we pass over this vast sea to possess it.

Therefore let us choose life, that we and our seed may live, by obeying His voice and cleaving to Him, for He is our life and our prosperity.[2]

A few days later, the fleet set sail for the new world. Winthrop's son Henry sailed with the fleet, but his wife and other children remained behind in England, waiting to join him in a later year. The crossing of the Atlantic was relatively uneventful and the fleet reached Massachusetts in early June of 1630. They stopped first at a small outpost established two years before in Salem, and then proceeded south to the larger harbor where the city of Boston is now found. The ships were disembarked and the colonists began establishing settlements on the shores of the bay and short distances up the several rivers that flowed into it. The largest was on a small peninsula that jutted into the bay and was named Charlestown, in honor of the King. About 200 of the 700 colonists settled there and began to build shelters. Things did not go well. The water supply was not adequate for the number, and many were ill from the voyage and were never able to recover their strength. Colonists began to die. After a few months, Winthrop and the others realized that their choice of location had been a mistake, and they moved across the Charles River's tidal estuary to a larger peninsula with much better supplies of fresh water. They named this settlement, Boston.

The Puritan colonists experienced the same difficulties as earlier settlers. The ocean crossing left them weak and probably malnourished. The summer months were hotter and more exhausting than what they were used to in England. And winter came earlier and was much colder than winters at home. Many died. Over 200 of the 700 who had crossed in Winthop's fleet, perished before the spring of 1631. They died of disease, starvation, and accidents. Winthrop's son Henry drowned attempting to swim across a river. Grim death struck Winthrop's family in England as well. His third son Forth unexpectedly took ill and died in November of

---

[2] Quotations taken from **A Model of Christian Charity**, found online at the website of The Winthrop Society, http://www.winthropsociety.com/doc_charity.php. Used by permission. Winthrop's metaphor of the Massachusetts colony as "a city set on a hill" has been used in speeches by John F. Kennedy, Ronald Reagan, Rudy Giuliani, and Sarah Palin.

1630. In April of 1631, Margaret gave birth to a daughter whom she named Anne. When the baby girl was five months old, Margaret and three of their six younger children set sail with the second fleet to join John. Sadly, little Anne died at sea, one week into the voyage.

The Puritan investors back in England continued their efforts to recruit additional colonists and to procure supplies to be sent to Massachusetts. The arrival of the first supply ship in March of 1631 ended the threat of starvation. Supply ships arrived each year thereafter, and the Puritans were much better supplied than the Pilgrims of Plymouth had been. The Puritans were much more successful at recruiting additional colonists as well. In all, over 20,000 Puritans came over from England between 1630 and 1640. The Puritan settlements in Massachusetts rapidly dwarfed the size of the Plymouth colony to the south.

John Winthrop was re-elected as governor of the colony for each of the first three years of its existence. He spent a great deal of time setting up the forms of government which had been familiar to him as a lawyer in England and as a member of the county commission for Suffolk. With over 500 colonists settled over a broad area, there were inevitably issues for the courts to deal with. Property and ownership disputes had to be resolved, and breaches of the peace had to be dealt with. Winthrop was usually the voice of moderation and leniency. In all cases he sought for reconciliation between embittered parties. In matters of religion, he encouraged each of the settlements to establish a church and appoint a minister. The ministers from the various settlements gathered and met together twice a month to discuss matters of religious practice and theology. When disputes arose, Winthrop encouraged patience and forbearance. These practices echoed Winthrop's experiences growing up and living in the godly community of the Stour valley back in England.

In the election of 1634, Winthrop was defeated, and Thomas Dudley, formerly lieutenant governor was elected as Governor. Dudley's main reason for running against Winthrop was that he felt he had been too lenient in enforcing the laws of the colony. Winthrop retained a position on the governing council, but freed of the day-to-day duties as governor he devoted himself to expanding his own farm, increasing the number of his cattle, and establishing ordinances and good government for the booming settlement of Boston. Over the next few years, Dudley's popularity decreased, and Winthrop's reputation rebounded. In 1636, he was elected deputy governor.

In 1637 the Puritan colony faced serious challenges. Within a year or two of the first settlements by the Puritans around Massachusetts Bay, some colonists were venturing further inland, as far as the Connecticut River valley. Those who sought to trade in furs knew that this was an area rich in beaver and the river served as an easy way for both English and Indians to bring their furs to market. In contrast to the abandoned villages of the Pawtuxets on the Bay, the Connecticut River valley and Narraganset Bay were dotted with Indian settlements, some large, some small. The chiefs of the rival tribes were usually interested in trading furs for English goods, but there were inevitably misunderstandings, flashes of temper, and occasionally, violence. The rival Indian tribes often competed in trying to recruit the English as allies in their clashes with each other. In 1636, the Pequot Indians in the Connecticut River valley attacked and killed several English fur traders. The Governor of Massachusetts, Henry Vane, demanded that the killers be turned over for trial in the English courts. The Pequots refused. In May, John Winthrop was elected Governor again. Winthrop ordered the militia to assemble and wrote to Governor Bradford of neighboring Plymouth and asked him to send his militia as well. Under the command of Captain John Mason, a veteran English soldier, approximately 90 English militia men from Massachusetts Bay and Plymouth marched on the Pequots. They attacked one of the main Pequot settlements and killed six or seven hundred Indians, not just warriors, but also women and children. The Pequots sued for peace. The Pequot chief fled west and sought refuge among the Mohawks (an Iroquois tribe). The Mohawks killed the Pequot chief and sent his scalp to Boston as proof of their friendship with the English. The Pequot war achieved the result sought by Winthrop and the council. The Massachusetts Bay colony had no more trouble with any of the surrounding Indian tribes for the next forty years.

In 1637 Governor Winthrop faced another crisis which threatened the peace of the Massachusetts Bay colony. A religious dispute split the colony into warring factions. The Massachusetts colony was organized by the emigrants from England on the pattern they had known at home. The parish was a geographic unit for both civil and religious government. Just as in England, there was only one church in each parish. In England, ministers (or priests) had been nominally appointed by bishops, although in many parts of England, local landowners still had the right to nominate a minister of their choice. In the Massachusetts Bay Colony, ministers were selected by a vote of the men in each congregation. Congregational control was the "New England model" for church government. The leaders of the colony were Puritans and they recruited Puritans in England each year to sell their houses and land and join the colony. Within the broad community of Puritans, though, there were differences of opinion on certain matters. One issue which loomed large at the time was the proper biblical understanding of "works" and "grace." All Puritans agreed that salvation was by grace, but they differed about the emphasis to be placed on "works." Some thought that those who had been saved would naturally be motivated to keep the law and live a righteous life. They believed that a righteous life was evidence that one had been saved. Other Puritans rejected this as a form of legalism. Some went so far as to maintain that a Christian saved by grace was no longer capable of sin, and so should not be concerned about an outward conformity to laws. They accused the Puritans who emphasized living a righteous life as preaching a "covenant of works." There were Puritans in each camp among those who came to Massachusetts throughout the 1630s. For the first few years, those of both opinions were able to maintain cordial relations in the parishes of the colony. But cordial relations eventually broke down.

William and Anne Hutchinson arrived with other Puritans in Massachusetts in 1634, four years after the settlements of Charlestown and Boston had been founded. Two years later, Anne's sister and brother-in-law, William and Mary Wheelwright arrived in Boston as well. Both the Hutchinsons and the Wheelwrights had been attracted to the preaching of the Rev. John Cotton. John Cotton was a Cambridge-educated Puritan minister who had been the leading preacher in the English port of Boston in Lincolnshire. Cotton had encouraged the Great Migration to Massachusetts, helped to organize it, and had preached to the colonists in Southampton before they left. It was not surprising when, four years later, facing charges by Archbishop Laud of non-conformity, he decided to leave England for Massachusetts.

In Boston, Anne Hutchinson quickly won the friendship and admiration of the other colonists. She was admitted to the church, and shortly thereafter began to host weekly meetings at her home to discuss the sermons. She continued her admiration for John Cotton, but became increasingly critical of the other pastor and preacher at the Boston church, the Rev. John Wilson. When her brother-in-law, the Rev. William Wheelwright arrived in Massachusetts in 1636, she urged that he be appointed as a third minister at the church in Boston. She was greatly disappointed when, instead, he was appointed as the minister in the smaller, neighboring town of Mount Wollaston (now Braintree). Her criticisms of Rev. Wilson and of the other ministers in the settlements around Boston became harsher. She pronounced that only Rev. Cotton and her brother-in-law, Rev. Wheelwright, truly preached a covenant of grace and that all the other ministers of the colony were preaching a covenant of works.

In December of 1636, the dispute between the two sides had become so unhappy that the General Court of the Colony called for a day of fasting, with public preaching, in hopes of reconciling the two factions. On January 17, 1637, Rev. Cotton preached in the morning on the need for peace and reconciliation. Rev. Wheelwright preached in the afternoon and charged that those who had branded him and his wife and his sister- and brother-in-law as antinomians were the greatest enemies to the state that can be. He urged that all who had the true spirit of godliness must prepare themselves for a spiritual combat. This made matters worse rather than better. In March of 1637, with Winthrop serving as deputy governor, the General Court judged Rev. Wheelwright to have been guilty of sedition, but sentence was postponed. The next month, Winthrop was elected governor for the first time since 1633. Behind the scenes, Winthrop did all he could to bring about reconciliation between Rev. Cotton, Rev. Wilson, and Rev. Wheelwright. In August, 1637, the first meeting of Massachusetts clergy was held, called a Synod. Cotton and

Wilson were reconciled. Wheelwright remained defiant and critical of the other ministers, denouncing them as heretics and not Christian. In November, 1637 the General Court dealt with the religious disputes by first banishing Wheelwright and a number of his supporters, and then

summoning Anne Hutchinson to answer for her remarks. She was charged with sedition for having denounced the ministers as "no true ministers because they preached a covenant of works." Hutchinson was bright and articulate and sparred with Governor Winthrop and the other members of the court, challenging them to indicate what law she had broken. At last, exasperated, she claimed that she knew, by "direct revelation of the Holy Spirit" who were the true ministers in the colony and who were not. Only Rev. Cotton and Rev. Wheelwright were true ministers she proclaimed. The court found her guilty of sedition and banished her from the colony, but gave her leave to remain through the winter until the spring. Over the winter, though confined to her house, she continued to receive visitors and to repeat her criticisms of the ministers and magistrates. In March of 1638, the Boston church ex-communicated her. In April, Anne and William Hutchinson left the Massachusetts colony and settled on an island in the Narragansett Bay which they had purchased from the Indians. After her husband died in 1642, Anne and her children moved further away, to the Dutch colony of New Amsterdam at the mouth of the Hudson River. She and her children were killed in an Indian attack in 1643.

In 1643, the Rev. William Wheelwright (who had moved north to New Hampshire with his wife) wrote a letter of apology to Winthrop and asked for help in having his sentence of banishment lifted. Winthrop wrote him a letter of safe conduct and saw to it that the General Court in 1644 lifted his banishment.

Meanwhile, back in Boston, the colony of Puritans prospered. In 1636, the General Court of the Massachusetts colony had agreed to contribute a substantial sum towards the establishment of a college. In 1637 Newtown was chosen as the site for the school and the next year, Newtown was renamed, Cambridge. In 1638, one of the wealthier colonists, Rev. John Harvard of Charlestown died, and left all of his library and half of his estate as an endowment for the college, which was promptly renamed in his honor.

From Boston, John Winthrop followed the political developments in England as closely as he could. The hopes of the colonists for reform in England rose when Parliament was summoned in 1640, and then were dashed when King Charles attempted to dissolve Parliament and finally withdrew to raise an army against it in 1642. When war broke out, a number of the colonists returned to England to fight in the Puritan / Parliamentary Army. When the English Parliament called for a religious assembly to draw up a new religious settlement for the Church of England, they extended invitations to three of the Massachusetts Bay clergy as well, though in the end, none attended.

Throughout the 1640s Winthrop served on the General Court. In 8 out of 12 annual elections from 1637 to 1648, he was elected governor (1637, 1638, 1639, 1642, 1643, 1646, 1647, and 1648). By 1647, all of Winthrop's surviving children had grown to adulthood and left home. His oldest, John Jr., now 41, was a prominent settler in New London, Connecticut. After John Sr.'s death, he would be elected governor of the colony of Connecticut. His son Stephen (his third wife, Margaret's eldest son), now 28, had returned to England and become an officer in the Parliamentary army in the civil war with King Charles. Adam, 27, and Deane, 24, had both established themselves as merchants and farmers, and Adam had recently married. Samuel, 20 had gone abroad to seek his fortune and ended up in Antigua in the Caribbean where he would, in time, become a prosperous sugar planter, with a plantation he named Groton Hall.

In June 1647, an "epidemical sickness" broke out throughout New England. Several hundred colonists died, including the Rev. Thomas Hooker. On June 14, Governor Winthrop made the following entry in his journal:

> "In this sickness the governor's wife, daughter of Sir John Tindal, Knight, left this world for a better, being about fifty-six years of age: a woman of singular virtue, prudence, modesty, and piety, and specially beloved and honored of all the country."

Governor Winthrop was now alone in his house in Boston, living with only a few servants. Six months after his third wife's death, he married again – to Martha Nowell Cotymore, who herself had been widowed three years before. One year later, John and Martha Winthrop became parents as Joshua Winthrop was born. Governor Winthrop was taken ill just two months after his youngest son's birth. His friends visited him and Rev. Cotton of the Boston church exhorted the congregation to pray for their governor. On March 26th, 1649 Governor John Winthrop of the Massachusetts Bay colony died at his home in Boston. He was 61 years old. He had lived in Old England for the first 42 years of his life, and in New England for the last 19. He had been elected governor for 12 of those 19 years. He left behind six surviving sons and a prosperous colony with a population which had grown from the initial 700 Puritans in the Winthrop Fleet of 1630 to over 15,000. Without his leadership, the colony might never have come into existence. With another governor they might have all perished or been reduced to anarchy or civil war.

Two hundred years later, Nathaniel Hawthorne, of Salem, Massachusetts would set one of the pivotal scenes of his novel **The Scarlet Letter**, on the night of Governor Winthrop's death:

> The good old minister [Rev. Wilson] came freshly from the death-chamber of Governor Winthrop, who had passed from earth to heaven within that very hour. And now, surrounded, like the saint-like personages of olden times, with a radiant halo, that glorified him amid this gloomy night of sin, -- as if the departed Governor had left him an inheritance of his glory, or as if he had caught upon himself the distant shine of the celestial city, while looking thitherward to see the triumphant pilgrim pass within its gates, -- now, in short, good Father Wilson was moving homeward, aiding his footsteps with a lighted lantern!

Blaise Pascal

1623-1662

courtesy of www.philippedechampaigne.org

Blaise Pascal was born in 1623 in the French city of Clermont, capitol of the Auvergne region of central France to Etienne and Antoinette Pascal.

His father was a local judge and a member of the nobility. Pascal's mother died when he was three. As a member of the nobility, and a former judicial official, Etienne had a large enough fortune that he could devote himself exclusively to the education of his children. When Pascal was eight, his father moved the small family to Paris. Gilberte, Blaise's older sister, was eleven and Jacqueline, his younger sister was six. Paris offered many more opportunities for his children than Clermont. Etienne was widely read and accomplished in both mathematics and natural science. He had long carried on a correspondence with several of the leading mathematicians in Paris, and as soon as he had settled there he began attending weekly meetings of a small circle of learned men who met at the residence of Father Mersenne, a catholic priest.

Etienne planned the education of his children very carefully. He was aware that his son, Pascal, was very bright – something of a prodigy. He wished his son to be well-rounded and wanted him to master composition and grammar in French, Latin, and Greek before beginning to study mathematics and the sciences. He planned to wait to introduce the study of geometry to his son until he was fifteen. Blaise had other ideas. Etienne surprised his twelve year old son one day while he was working on geometrical figures and problems. Etienne was astonished to discover that Blaise had worked out many of the principles of geometry on his own. He was quickly persuaded to relax his rule and allowed Blaise to continue his study of mathematics. He gave young Blaise a copy of Euclid and invited him to begin attending the weekly meetings at Father Mersenne.

The meetings at Father Mersenne's, while informal, put Blaise at the center of mathematical and scientific thought in the 1600s. Marin Mersenne, born in 1588, had studied at the Sorbonne as a classmate with Rene Descartes. He had written numerous books and pamphlets on mathematics, natural science, theology and music. He maintained a correspondence with learned men all over Europe. He enjoyed meeting with other learned men and discussing and debating the latest scientific theories and advances in mathematics. The group of scholars who met with him would later form the nucleus of the French Royal Academy of Science. It was this august gathering that Blaise began attending with his father when he was twelve.

When Blaise was fifteen, he wrote an essay on a difficult topic in geometry, "conic sections." Father Mersenne was astonished at the original insights and proofs which Blaise wrote about. He sent a copy of the manuscript to his friend Descartes, who refused to belief that the author was a boy of fifteen.

In 1638, Etienne's investment in royal bonds was suddenly and arbitrarily devalued by an act of King Louis XIII. When Etienne joined others in writing a formal petition and remonstrance, Richelieu issued an order for his arrest and imprisonment. Etienne was warned and was able to flee Paris and go into hiding in the country. He left his three children in the care of a governess in Paris and continued to provide funds for their education. Blaise continued his study of mathematics. His sisters studied literature. His younger sister, Jacqueline developed into an excellent poet, and an actress. In 1639, she appeared in a private performance of a play by Corneille attended by Cardinal Richelieu. Her performance impressed the Cardinal and he invited her to make of him any request she wished. She immediately asked for a pardon for her father. The Cardinal kept his promise extravagantly. He invited Etienne Pascal and his three children to be his guests at his chateau in the country for a weekend. He then appointed Etienne as the King's Commissioner of Taxes in the city of Rouen. For the next six years, Blaise assisted his father in Rouen with his duties as the Tax Commissioner.

In 1646, Etienne had a serious accident which dislocated his hip and forced him to remain in bed for many months. His recovery was doubtful, and Blaise and his father turned to two aristocratic brothers, Monsieur de la Bouteilerie and Monsieur des Landes who had a reputation for great skill in caring for the sick and injured. They were also devoted Christians who belonged to a Catholic movement called the Jansenists, named after an influential Catholic priest, Father Cornelius Jansen. Jansen emphasized the debilitating effects of original sin, the necessity of grace, and predestination. Jansen cited the works of the great early church father, St. Augustine in support of his views. To many of his catholic critics, Jansen's ideas sounded suspiciously like those of John Calvin.

The two brothers took excellent care of Etienne. They also sought to care for the souls of the Pascals, and gave them pamphlets by Father Jansen to read. Blaise was struck by how much sense they made, and chagrined to think of how much time he had wasted on frivolous and worldly pursuits. He resolved to devote his life to serving God and seeking His truth, and to forgo the accumulation of wealth or fame for himself. Etienne and Jacqueline were also persuaded. His older sister Gilbert had married several years before, but when she and her husband came for a visit to Rouen, they too resolved to join in devoting their lives to serving God.

In 1647, Blaise and Jacqueline moved back to Paris, at least partly in order to be close to the Paris convent of Port-Royal, which was the center of the Jansenists in France. Pascal visited the convent and the school connected with it frequently.

Paris in the 1640s was a city in turmoil. Cardinal Richelieu had died in 1642. King Louis XIII died in 1643. The new king, Louis XIV was only five years old when his father died. The government of France was directed by his mother Queen Anne of Austria, and her chief minister, Cardinal Mazarin. In 1648, the Cardinal arrested the leaders of the city council in Paris who had been refusing to pay new taxes imposed in the name of the King. This provoked a popular uprising that was quickly joined by a faction of dissident nobles, who demanded a meeting of the Etats-general (the French Parliament) which had not been assembled since 1615. Anne, Cardinal Mazarin, and Louis had to flee the city to escape being attacked and captured by angry French peasants. It took only a few months for the royal army, to return from service in Germany and restore order in Paris, but the experience proved quite frightening to the young Louis XIV – it remained his most vivid childhood memory.

When the riots of the Fronde broke out, Blaise and Jacqueline fled from Paris back to their ancestral home in Clermont, where their older sister Gilberte and her husband Florin Perier were living. When peace was restored, they returned to Paris.

In 1651, Etienne Pascal, Blaise's father died. Within a few months, Jacqueline entered the convent of Port Royal in Paris and took vows as a nun. Blaise was now on his own. He was 28 and, thanks to his inheritance, quite well off. He was well known in scientific circles throughout France and much of the rest of Europe as a brilliant mathematician and natural scientist. Pascal spent the next few years enjoying the life of a nobleman in Paris. He was well-known, admired, wealthy, a scholar, and a scientist. As a hobby, he spent some time analyzing the mathematics of gambling, and laid the foundation for the modern study of statistics in a series of letters to a friend – though he does not seem to have been much of a gambler himself.

In 1654, Pascal was jolted from his life of ease and complacency. His biographers are still unclear about the details, but when Pascal died a piece of paper was found sewn into his coat which begins:

In the year of Grace, 1654,
On Monday, 23rd of November . . .
From about half past ten in the evening until about half past twelve
    FIRE
God of Abraham, God of Isaac, God of Jacob, not of philosophers and scholars.
Certainty, Certainty. Feeling. Joy. Peace.
God of Jesus Christ.

Blaise resumed his close relationship with the Jansenists at the convent of Port Royal. But the Jansenists were controversial. The Catholic establishment of France had never been happy with them. Richelieu had attacked the convent and tried to close it down. The Jesuits accused the Jansenists of flirting with Protestant heresy. In 1656, the Jesuits succeeded in having the leader of Jansentists in France, Father Antoine Arnauld condemned by the theology faculty of the Sorbonne.

In response to this attack, Pascal wrote a series of eighteen letters which were issued as anonymous pamphlets every few weeks over a period of 14 months, each with the title "Letter from the Provinces." Pascal's writing was brilliant. It was simple, funny, and scathing in its critique of the Jesuits and its defense of the Jansenists. The letters were wildly popular. Their style has been widely admired and is often used as an example of the best of French literature. King Louis the XIV was furious. He ordered the letters destroyed and sought, unsuccessfully, to discover who had written them.

The Provincial Letters proved popular, but they were unable to rescue the Jansenists or the convent and school at Port Royal. The school was ordered closed and the nuns were ordered to sign letters condemning the heretical doctrines of Cornelius Jansen. Pascal's sister, Jacqueline, refused for many months, and then died of tuberculosis in October of 1661.

Blaise now devoted all his time to writing a new book which he titled **A Defense of Christianity**, but his health was poor as well. His sister, Gilberte came to Paris to look after him, but he died in August, 1662 without finishing the great work he was working on. After his death, his notes were collected and organized as the **Thoughts of Pascal on Religion** (in French, the **Pensées**).

Rembrandt Harmensz van Rijn

1606 – 1669

Rembrandt van Rijn was born in 1606 in the Dutch city of Leiden. This was the same Dutch city where the Pilgrims under the leadership of Pastor John Robinson and Elder William Brewster settled for twelve years, from 1608 to 1620. The English separatists arrived when Rembrandt was two, and left for the new world when he was twelve. Though there is no evidence for it, it is intriguing to speculate on whether they ever crossed paths. Who knows what a Dutch lad of nine or ten would have made of the English Pilgrims?

Rembrandt's father was a miller and his family were prosperous and solid citizens. They owned a house in town, and a farm in the country. When Rembrandt was seven, he began attending the Latin School in Leiden, in preparation for admission to the University. He entered the University when he was fourteen, though there were already signs that he was more interested in painting than in anything else. At fifteen, his parents apprenticed him to a painter in Leiden, Jacob van Swanenburgh. He spent three years learning the craft of portrait painting and quickly surpassed in skill his master and teacher. When he was eighteen, Rembrandt spent six months working in the studio of Pieter Lastman in Amsterdam and then returned to Leiden, opened his own studio, and began to accepting commissions. Over the next five years, he earned a reputation as a gifted painter whose portraits were astonishing in their warmth and skill. His fame grew, first in Leiden, then in the other cities of the Netherlands. In 1629, his paintings came to the attention of Constantijn Huygens, poet, musician, diplomat, and personal secretary to Prince Frederick of Orange, the hereditary ruler of the Netherlands. Huygens recommended Rembrandt to members of the Dutch Court and Rembrandt began to receive a number of very well-paying commissions.

There is a remarkable self-portrait of Rembrandt, painted in 1630, when he was 24, still living in the home of his parents, but already working in his own studio. It shows a confident young man, who stares directly at the viewer, with an air of serenity and pride. The hair is painted in broad strokes, but the lace at his collar and the red shirt under a dark black jacket are done in precise detail. The facial features are clear and distinct, and there is a strong contrast between the right side of the face, in bright sunlight, and the left side, in shadow.

With his reputation beginning to spread, Rembrandt decided in 1631 to move from Leiden to Amsterdam, a much larger city. He established a studio in a house owned by an art dealer, and continued painting portraits and seeking commissions.

He was industrious, averaging a finished oil painting every month, year in and year out. Scholars now believe there are at least 300 (some say 600) oil paintings by Rembrandt still in existence, painted over his forty year career. In 1632, the young Rembrandt received his first large, public commission. Each year, the Amsterdam city council permitted one anatomy lesson using the body of an executed criminal. Dr. Tulp had recently been elected as Professor of Anatomy by the Amsterdam guild of surgeons. He wished for the yearly anatomy lesson (and himself of course) to be commemorated by a large oil painting. The twenty-six year old Rembrandt produced a masterpiece. It is a large canvas, almost six feet tall and over seven feet

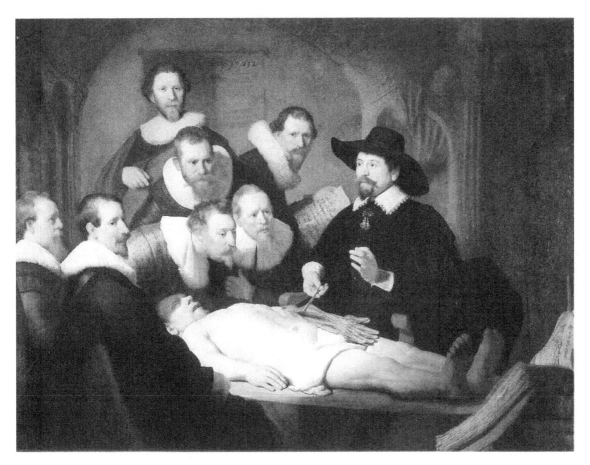

wide. It is a masterful treatment of a complex scene. Dr Tulp is, of course, the most prominent figure, but other doctors (who presumably also paid the artist a commission) are also included with a range of interested expressions. The shadow on the cadaver's face is in sharp contrast to the bright shafts of light that illuminate his torso, and the faces of the doctors. The painting was completely different from the static, posed group portraits which were being done by other artists. The demand for paintings, especially portraits, by the young Rembrandt soared. Over the next two years, he painted forty portraits.

Two years later, when he was 28, Rembrandt married Saskia van Uylenburg. He also became a citizen of the city of Amsterdam, and a member of the local guild of painters. Saskia gave birth to a son in 1635, a daughter in 1638, and a second daughter in 1640, but sadly all of the children died within a few weeks of being born. Only their fourth child, Titus, born in 1641, survived, eventually becoming a painter alongside his father.

In 1639, Rembrandt and Saskia bought a prominent house in Amsterdam, in a part of Amsterdam with a large Jewish community. The Netherlands was unique at the time in Europe in offering safety and refuge to those fleeing religious persecution. As a result, not only English separatists, but also Jews from the rest of Europe, especially Spain and parts of Germany moved to the Netherlands where they were safe and where they quickly joined the local economy as merchants and prospered.

In 1642, Rembrandt completed his second, public monumental masterpiece. The painting is titled *The Company of Frans Banning Cocq and Willem van Ruytenburch.* Rembrandt had been commissioned by the members of the city militia to paint a large group portrait. Other Dutch artists did these commissions by posing the members of the group in a stiff motionless arrangement. Rembrandt's painting is dramatically different. First, it is huge. It is a canvas that is almost 12 feet tall, and over 14 feet wide.

Instead of a posed group, it shows the Captain and the members of his company as they are about to sortie out from their armory, carrying weapons and in uniform. There are several dramatic lighting effects which single out particular persons. There is also an astonishing sense of motion as the Captain and his second-in-command seem to almost stride off the canvas towards the viewer. Rembrandt was paid a commission of over $10,000 for this painting and it hung prominently in the armory of the city militia.

Although painted as a daytime scene, soon after Rembrandt completed the gigantic canvas a layer of varnish was added to protect the original painting. This varnish gradually turned dark and within a generation or so the whole scene had become so dark that it came to be called the "Nightwatch." It was not until the 1970s that museum curators restored the painting, removed the layers of varnish and allowed it to be seen once again as Rembrandt had painted it.

In addition to his portraits, Rembrandt was commissioned to paint a number of scenes from the Bible and from mythology. Prince Frederick of Orange commissioned six paintings of scenes from the life of Christ. Other purchasers commissioned paintings telling the stories of Abraham and Samson.

In 1642, a few months after Titus' birth, Saskia died. Rembrandt grieved for his wife, and for his lost children. He doted on Titus and took pains to arrange for constant care for him. He painted less in the 1640s. One of his frequent subjects was the Holy Family of Jesus, Mary & Joseph. In this composition, from 1645, the look of concern and care on Mary's face and the peaceful sleep of Jesus cannot help but remind us of his loss of Saskia and his deep affection for Titus. The figure of Joseph, hard at work in the background makes us think of Rembrandt himself, often at work for long hours in his studio – apart from his family in order to provide for them.

Sadly, Rembrandt proved a poor businessman and unable to keep track of or discipline his own expenses. He often bought paintings he liked at auctions and collected works of art and curios that he would impulsively purchase at high prices. He stopped making payments on the mortgage on the house that he and Saskia had bought and finally, in 1656, his creditors and the mortgage-holder foreclosed on him. His personal collection of paintings was inventoried and sold to satisfy his debts and he had to leave the house he had lived in for 19 years.

By 1660, when Titus turned 18, he and Rembrandt's long-time housekeeper, Hendrickje Stoffels took over control of his financial affairs. By now, many of the older patrons who had supported Rembrandt had died or turned their attention to younger, newer artists. He was no longer quite so famous, nor so much in demand. There were still a few wealthy patrons who remembered when he had been the young prodigy, the miller's son from Leiden, but not many. In 1662, Rembrandt received his last great public commission. The six syndics (directors) of the cloth guild wished for a group portrait. The resulting painting is perhaps the most famous and recognizable of Rembrandt's works. The composition of six figures does not portray a sense of motion the way that the Nightwatch does, but they are far from static. They look as though they had been interrupted from some serious deliberation or examination of accounts and have all turned their attention toward the viewer, with an air of expectancy, wishing to know what important business has now come to be presented to them.

The faces are distinct, and with an air of nobility. The eyes catch our attention and draw us from one figure to the next. Each seems completely aware that he is a member of a larger group, and yet quite confident of his position and giving the new matter his complete attention.

The details of chair, table, tablecloth, and carved wood-paneling are carefully depicted, without being distracting.

Rembrandt continued his painting through the 1660s, but his health was beginning to fail and he wasn't able to see his subjects as clearly. Yet, even now, he continued to produce stunning paintings on a variety of themes. Each year, he painted at least one self-portrait.

Here are two. The first is from 1661, when he was 55 years old. The second is from 1669, when he was 63, and completed just a few months before his death. Sadly, his son Titus died in an outbreak of the plague which swept through the Netherlands in 1668. Rembrandt, no longer famous, no longer in demand, no longer rich, died in October 1669.

John Milton

1608-1674

John Milton was born in London in 1608. His father and mother were well-off and well-educated. His father, John Milton, Sr. was a notary and financier. In 1620, he was named a trustee of Blackfriars Theatre, which was the winter quarters of the King's Men (whose most famous member had been the actor and playwright, William Shakespeare). When the first folio of Shakespeare's plays was published in 1623, John Milton Sr. contributed a poem on Shakespeare which was included in the introduction. Shakespeare died when Milton was eight. It is not known whether they ever met, but it is certainly possible, though Milton never mentions any personal encounter.

The Miltons owned two houses in London, as well as a house in the country. John Sr.'s business dealings were conducted from offices on the ground floor of a five story building in the center of London. The family lived on the other four floors. In addition to his work as a notary and financier, John Sr. also composed music for madrigals and for the singing of the Psalms. The Miltons were Puritan in their religion. The church they attended, All Hallows-Bread Street, was only a short walk down the street from the building where they lived. The minister and practices at the church were decidedly Puritan in all their details.

John Sr. arranged for a private tutor to teach his children (John Jr. had an older sister, and a younger brother) to read and write and the basics of arithmetic. At seven John, Jr. began to study Latin, which was required for admission to the best private schools, and for university.

When he was twelve, Milton began attending the prestigious St. Paul's school. Like All Hallows Church, the school was only a few blocks away from the Milton's home. The young Milton excelled at everything having to do with languages and literature. Milton later described his school years this way: "I had so keen an appetite for the study of literature that from my twelfth year scarcely ever did I leave my studies for my bed before the hour of midnight." At St. Paul's all students were thoroughly instructed in Greek, Latin, and Hebrew. All instruction was given in Latin and students were required to speak only Latin while in school. In addition to the study of classical languages at St. Paul's, Milton's father encouraged and instructed him at home in French and Italian, both of which he mastered.

After four years at St. Paul's, Milton left London to enroll as a student at Cambridge University. His plan was to prepare himself for ordination as a minister in the Church of England. He continued his study of languages and literature at Cambridge, while also taking courses in theology. He wrote poetry in English and in Latin, and a few Petrarchan sonnets in Italian. During the 1620s, Milton became discouraged about the prospect of becoming a minister. The leadership of the Church of England under James and Charles, especially Bishop Laud, was increasingly hostile to the Puritan faction. Milton did not think that any Bishop would be likely to ordain him or appoint him to pastor a parish. He saw little chance of a career in the church.

It was dangerous to be out of favor with the King and his Bishops. In 1628, one of Milton's teachers from St. Paul's, Alexander Gil, wrote some foolhardy verses celebrating the assassination of the Duke of Buckingham (a friend of King Charles, and before that the favorite of King James). Gil was degraded from the ministry, stripped of his Oxford degrees, fined £2,000 and sentenced to have both ears cut off. The King reduced the sentence and Gil kept his ears, but he spent two years in prison, before King Charles finally pardoned him. For Milton and other Puritans in England it was one more sign that Charles was a tyrant.

In March of 1629, Milton received his Bachelor's degree from Cambridge. He remained at Cambridge and began working towards a Master's degree, which he finished 3 years later in

1632. Now 24 years old, with no prospects for appointment in the Church of England, Milton returned home to live with his parents. His father, 70 years old, had retired from business in London and moved to the suburb of Hammersmith. Because of his family's wealth, Milton did not have to seek employment. He was free to pursue his love of literature and to develop his skills as a writer and a poet.

> "At my father's country place, whither he had retired to spend his declining years, I devoted myself entirely to the study of Greek and Latin writers, completely at leisure, not, however without sometimes exchanging the country for the city, either to purchase books, or to become acquainted with some new discovery in mathematics or music, in which I then took the keenest pleasure."

In 1637, Milton's mother died. Shortly thereafter, Milton decided he should embark on a "grand tour" of France and Italy. He left in May of 1638, and returned to England in August of 1639. In France, he visited only Paris, before traveling on to Italy via Nice and Genoa, arriving in Florence in July of 1638. He spent several months in Florence, admiring the art and the atmosphere. While there, he visited the astronomer Galileo, under house-arrest for his defense of Copernicus, and already well-known in England. In September, he journeyed on to Rome, where he stayed for seven months (with one brief excursion to Naples). In the spring of 1639, he traveled to Venice and then to Geneva, returning home to London via Paris at the end of the summer. Back in London, he moved in with his older sister and became tutor to her children, two boys (now aged nine and eight) and two girls.

In 1640, King Charles was forced by the defeat of his army by the Scots to call for the election of a new Parliament. No Parliament had met for eleven years. It quickly became apparent that the Puritans, disapproved of by Charles and persecuted by Bishop Laud were going to be the majority party. The king's chief advisor, Strafford, was attainted by act of Parliament and executed. Archbishop Laud was likewise deposed from his office and imprisoned in the Tower of London. Milton, living in London, was drawn into Parliamentary politics and began writing pamphlets in the heated debate over the proper form of church government. Milton's name began to be well-known as an articulate spokesman for the Puritan cause.

In 1643, at the age of 35, Milton married Mary Powell, 17, of Forest Hill, Oxfordshire. Her father had been a client and business associate of his father's. We know very little about their courtship. But we do know that something went wrong in the first few weeks of the marriage. After a month, Mary left Milton in London and returned to her parent's home. Milton responded by composing a tract on divorce. In the tract, Milton argues that divorce by mutual consent for incompatibility is not forbidden by the Bible. He argues that the main purpose of marriage is mutual companionship and that if this be not possible, then no true marriage can exist. Other Puritans reacted strongly. Milton and his tract on divorce were condemned and he found himself denounced from Puritan pulpits.

In London, Milton continued as a tutor to his nephews, and began to take on additional students as well. As the number of his students increased, what began as private instruction gradually evolved into a school. In 1644, Milton wrote and published a pamphlet defending the liberty of unlicensed printing and arguing against the censorship of books. The essay was titled **Areopagitica** – a reference to the Areopogus of Athens where Greek orators delivered speeches and debated public policy. Milton argues that neither Greek nor Roman society ever practiced censorship over political or philosophical writings. He argued that the best antidote to pernicious writing was not to ban it, but to argue with it, and refute it with the truth. "Who ever knew Truth put to the worse in a free and open encounter?" He further argues that the power of censorship is among the most abused by tyrants. The essay ends with an eloquent plea: *"Give me the liberty to know, to utter, and to argue freely according to conscience, above all liberties."*

In June of 1645, the Puritans won their decisive victory over King Charles at Naseby and the civil war was all but over. The Puritans and Parliament had won. London, which was overwhelmingly Puritan rejoiced. Later that summer, a relative of Milton's invited him to pay a call. When Milton arrived, he found Mary Powell Milton, his estranged wife, in the parlor, on her knees, making submission, and begging his pardon. Milton was at first reluctant to agree to a reconciliation, but could not hold out for long. Mary joined him as his wife in his home in

London and remained with him as his wife until her death in 1652. They had four children, 3 daughters and a son, who died as an infant.

In January of 1646, Milton published his first volume of poetry. Half of the poems were in English, the other half in Latin. In the summer of 1646, the Parliamentary army occupied Oxford and Mary Powell Milton's family (who were Royalist in their sympathies) had to flee their home. John Milton offered them shelter at his house in London. His father- and mother-in-law along with several of his wife's younger siblings moved into the house which already housed a number of students from Milton's private school, as well as John Sr., Milton's 83 year old father.

In early 1647 Milton's father and father-in-law both died. In settling the estates of both men, Milton was able to find separate quarters for his in-laws, and to purchase a new residence for himself and his wife and daughters. He closed the school. In January, 1649 the court appointed by Parliament found King Charles I guilty of treason and had him executed. Two weeks later, Milton published a pamphlet defending the concept of a limited monarchy and the right of subjects to depose a tyrant or wicked king. Shortly thereafter, he accepted an appointment as "Secretary for Foreign Tongues" to the Committee of Foreign Affairs which was in turn a subset of the Council of State which then governed England. His duties were to handle all of the correspondence to and from foreign governments.

Within weeks of King Charles' execution, a book with the title ***Eikon Basilike* or The King's Book** appeared (*Eikon Basilike* is Greek for *image of the king*). The book presented itself as being written by Charles himself, defending his actions in the recent civil war. The book generated great sympathy for the dead King. Milton was commissioned by the Council of Staate to write a reply. He worked carefully for seven months on an essay entitled ***Eikonoklastes*** (which means the *image breaker*). It was not his best work, but he was forced into a format in which he answered the points and charges of the **Eikon Basilike** point by point without the freedom to write an essay on his own terms.

After Milton's essay was published, a French scholar published **Defensio Regia pro Carolo I.** Once again, the Council of State commissioned Milton to write a reply. Milton titled his reply, **Pro Populo Anglicano Defensio**. This essay succeeded better and won for Milton a reputation as a brilliant essayist outside of England for the first time.

One year later, Milton had completely lost his sight. The development was not completely unexpected – his vision had been failing for several years, but it was devastating to him nonetheless. The Council of State thought so highly of his abilities that they kept him in office and now provided him with an assistant to read to him and a secretary to write down for him all that he wished to compose. In the same year that he lost his sight, he also lost his wife. Mary Powell Milton died in May of 1652 from complications following childbirth. Milton was now blind, and a widower with three small daughters. But he continued to work as the foreign secretary of the Republic under the rule of Oliver Cromwell, who took the title, "Protector of the Realm." From 1657 to 1659, Milton's assistant was the poet Andrew Marvell, who was also master of Latin, French, Italian, and Spanish. Sometime after his blindness, he composed the following sonnet:

Sonnet 19

When I consider how my light is spent,
  E're half my days, in this dark world and wide
  And that one Talent which is death to hide,
  Lodg'd with me useless, though my Soul more bent
To serve therewith my Maker, and present
  My true account, lest he returning chide,
  "Doth God exact day labour, light deny'd,"
  I fondly ask; But patience to prevent
That murmur, soon replies, "God doth not need
  Either man's work or his own gifts, who best
  Bear his mild yoke, they serve him best, his State
Is Kingly. Thousands at his bidding speed
  And post o're Land and Ocean without rest:
  They also serve who only stand and wait."

In 1656, four years after the death of his first wife, Milton married for a second time. Fifteen months later, Katherine Woodcock Milton died from complications of childbirth. Milton grieved deeply for her, and composed and dictated the following sonnet:

Sonnet 23

Methought I saw my late espoused Saint
   Brought to me like Alcestis from the grave,
   Whom Jove's great son to her glad Husband gave,
   Rescu'd from death by force though pale and faint.
Mine as whom washt from spot of child-bed taint,
   Purification in the old Law did save,
   And such, as yet once more I trust to have
   Full sight of her in Heaven without restraint,
Came vested all in white, pure as her mind:
   Her face was veil'd, yet to my fancied sight,
   Love, sweetness, goodness, in her person shin'd
So clear, as in no face with more delight.
   But O as to embrace me she inclin'd,
   I wak'd, she fled, and day brought back my night.

In September of 1658, Oliver Cromwell died and his son Richard was named as the new Protector. Richard had never served in the Army and they forced his resignation within the year. Representatives of the army then began negotiating with Charles II, in exile in France and made arrangements for him to return and be crowned as king. Through all of the political chaos, Milton continued to discharge his duties as Secretary for Foreign Tongues. As Charles returned, triumphant to England, Milton went into hiding.

The Restoration Parliament chose the curious tactic of limiting retribution for the death of Charles I to twenty men. After settling on a number, they debated who to put on the list. Milton was a candidate, but, in the end, there were twenty men whom Charles and the Royalists hated more than Milton, and he was spared. But many of those who were executed had been his friends and colleagues.

Milton retired to a small house in London, which he shared with his three daughters and several servants – all of whom spent hours reading to him, and taking dictation from him as he turned his attention entirely to literature. There was some lingering resentment between Milton and his daughters. Their relations were not cordial, though they continued to share the house with him. Some of Milton's friends were alarmed when they discovered that the daughters were selling the books from Milton's library to raise pocket-money for themselves. In 1663, one of Milton's long-time friends, Dr. Paget arranged a marriage for him. Milton was 55. His bride, Elizabeth Minshull was 25. She was described as a "genteel person, a peaceful and agreeable woman." We know from the description of other friends that Milton enjoyed listening to her sing while he accompanied her on a small house-organ on which he had developed some skill.

During the 1660s, Milton was at work continuing the composition of an epic poem – a project he had long had in mind, and had worked fitfully on, but had often postponed while employed in the service of the Protectorate. He spent hours each day dictating new lines which he had composed and memorized. When he completed his dictation, he would have previous pages read back to him so that he could revise them. In 1667, it was ready for publication. **Paradise Lost** is an epic account of the fall of man. It tells the story of Adam and Eve, their temptation in the garden, and their expulsion. It also tells the story of Lucifer's rebellion and expulsion from heaven. Though published in one volume, the poem was divided into twelve books (an echo of Virgil's **Aeneid**) and contains over 10,000 lines of verse. Milton's contemporaries immediately proclaimed it a masterpiece and placed Milton in the ranks of the great epic poets Homer and Virgil. The first printing sold out in less than 20 months

Four years later, Milton published a second epic poem, entitled **Paradise Regained**. In four books, totaling 2,000 lines Milton retells the story of the Temptation of Jesus in the wilderness from the gospel of Luke. The action forms a counter-point to **Paradise Lost** which focuses on the Adam and Eve's failure to resist the temptation of the devil. Jesus' successful resistance of his own temptation is the redemption of their failure. **Paradise Regained** did not receive the same critical acclaim as **Paradise Lost**, which frustrated and annoyed Milton. With **Paradise Regained**, Milton also published a short epic retelling of another biblical story, the death of Samson. Titled **Samson Agonistes**, this poem opens with the blind Samson as a slave in

Gaza and ends, 1758 lines later after an account of the destruction of the Philistine temple which kills the Philistine king and his nobles, along with Samson. In between there is a lengthy passage where Delilah approaches Samson and seeks his forgiveness. Samson forbids her to approach or touch him and only grudgingly says, "At distance I forgive thee, go with that."

In the early 1670s, Milton's friends arranged for a new publication of his collected poetry. All of his poems from the 1645 volume were reprinted, along with eight or nine others which had not appeared in print.

John Milton died on November 8th, 1674 at the age of 65. In spite of his Puritan views on religion and his service to Cromwell, out of favor now with the restoration of King Charles II, his public funeral drew a large crowd. His 3rd wife and widow, Elizabeth Milton outlived him by 53 years, and died in 1727.

Johannes Vermeer

1632-1675

Johannes Vermeer was born in 1632 in Delft. A few days after his birth, he was baptized at the Reformed Protestant church. His parents, Reynier and Digna Vermeer owned an inn at the market square in the center of Delft. Johannes and his sister, Gertruy, grew up helping their parents take care of the guests at the inn. But the inn was not the only source of income for the Vermeers. Reynier also bought and sold paintings and arranged commissions with the local artists in Delft. Delft had a population of about 15,000 when Vermeer lived there – about half the size of Amsterdam or Utrecht, but not too different from Leiden or Haarlem. Delft was an important city for the House of Orange, the noble family which ruled over the Netherlands. William I had been buried there in 1584, in the "New Church" and from that time on all of his descendants were laid to rest in a royal crypt which was built in the church.

In 1652, Johannes' father, Reynier died, and Johannes inherited ownership of his father's inn on the market. The next year, a few months before he turned 21, he married Catharina Bolnes, whose family was part of the Roman Catholic minority in Delft. Eight months after his wedding, Vermeer was admitted to the painter's guild in Delft, which gave him the right to offer his paintings for sale, and also to continue his father's business as an art dealer.

Over the next 22 years, he only painted thirty-four oil paintings (perhaps 35). Half of them were bought by Pieter and Maria van Ruijven, the wealthiest citizens of Delft. The others were almost all commissioned and bought by the merchants and burghers of Delft. A few were used to pay debts incurred by Vermeer and his family. During the 22 years that he was painting, Johannes and Catharina had fourteen children, though three of them died in infancy.

Other than his birth, marriage, and death, we know remarkably little about the details of Vermeer's life. We have nothing written by him. The only record left by his wife is her plea to the court trying to settle his estate. She begs for time to settle his debts as he left behind eleven children whom she has to care for. We do know that Vermeer was in Delft at significant points in the town's history. In 1647, when he was 15, Prince Frederick Henry of Nassau was given a large, public, state funeral in Delft. In 1660, King Charles II of England made a visit to Delft and was welcomed and entertained by the Burghermeister and town council.

In 1654, there was a violent explosion in Delft which killed over a hundred people and injured thousands and caused widespread damage in the center of town. The powderhouse, where gunpowder for the city militia was stored, located just off the central market, had exploded. There was nothing left of the house and every building near the market was extensively damaged by the blast. Vermeer likely was there. It is certain that the Inn was damaged. But we do not know a single detail of how it might have affected him.

We do know that Vermeer was elected as President of the Painters' Guild four times: in 1662 when he was 30, and also in 1663, 1670, and 1671.

1672 was a year of disaster for the Netherlands. Although the independence of the Netherlands from Spain had been recognized at the Peace of Westphalia in 1648, her neighbors had always peered at the provinces with a covetous eye. In 1672, the French under Louis XIV invaded the Netherlands from the South. France was joined and supported by the English, whose fleet attacked the ships of Dutch merchants, and by two German prince-electors. The Dutch army was defeated and most of the seven provinces were conquered and occupied. The Dutch rallied and halted the French army by flooding their fields and defending their besieged cities. In a few months, the French army was forced to withdraw. But the economy of the

Netherlands was wrecked. In the following winter there was widespread starvation. With the economy in such poor shape, no one had money to purchase paintings. Vermeer was forced to borrow large sums of money and the family ran up large bills with the Delft merchants.

In 1675, at the age of 43, Vermeer became despondent over his debts. His health collapsed, and he died after a short illness. He left behind a widow, eleven children, enormous debts, and thirty-four beautiful paintings.

The Houses of Stuart and Hannover
1603-1901

James I
born 1566
King 1603-1625

Anne
of Denmark

Prince Henry
1594-1612

Princess Elizabeth
1596-1662

Frederick V
Elector Palatine

Charles I
born 1600
King 1625-1649

Henrietta Maria
of France
1609-1669

12 children

Sophia
1630-1714

Ernst August
Elector of **Hannover**

Charles II
born 1630
King 1660-1685

Catherine
of Portugal

Mary
1631-1660

William II
of Orange
1626-1650

James II
born 1633
King 1685-1688
died 1701

(1) Anne Hyde
1638-1671

(2) Maria
of Modena

Illegitimate

James Scott
1649-1685
Duke of Monmouth

William III
born 1650
King 1688-1702

Mary
born 1662
Queen 1688-1694

Anne
born 1665
Queen 1702-1714

James Stuart
1688-1766
the Old Pretender

Maria
Sobieska

George I
born 1660
King 1714-1727

Sophia Dorothea
of Celle

Charles Stuart
1720-1788
the Young Pretender

Henry Stuart
1725-1807
Cardinal Duke of York

George II
born 1683
King 1727-1760

Caroline
of Ansbach

Prince Frederick
1707-1751

Augusta
of Saxe-Gotha

George III
born 1738
King 1760-1820

Charlotte
of Mecklenburg

George IV
born 1762
King 1820-1830

Caroline
of Brunswick

Frederick
1763-1827

Frederica
of Prussia

William IV
born 1765
King 1830-1837

Adelaide
of Saxe-Meiningen

Edward
1767-1820

Victoria
of Saxe-Coburg

Victoria
born 1819
Queen 1837-1901

Charles II

Born 1630, King from 1660 to 1685

James II

Born 1633, King from 1687 to 1688, Died 1701

Charles & James Stuart

On the 29th of May, 1630, Queen Henrietta Maria and King Charles I of England welcomed a son into the world. They had been married for five years. Their first child had been stillborn in 1629 and in 1630, with her second pregnancy, there was great concern for Henrietta Maria's health and the health of the baby. The King and Queen were much relieved when Charles proved a strong and healthy child. Charles was soon joined by a sister, Mary (born in 1631) and a brother, James (born in 1633). By 1644 Charles and Henrietta had six surviving children – three sons and three daughters. Charles was fifteen when his youngest sibling, a sister named Henrietta Anne was born. By then, of course, England was in the midst of a civil war between King and Parliament. When the war broke out, Queen Henrietta left for France with the four younger children. Charles and James stayed with their father and attended him at many of the military actions of the war. In 1646, his father feared for his safety and sent Charles away, with his own council of advisors, to rally support in the western counties. James stayed in Oxford, which served as the King's headquarters. When King Charles I was defeated and made a prisoner of Parliament in 1646, Charles and James both fled England. Charles made his way to France to join his mother in exile there. James went to Holland to join his sister, Mary, who had just married William II, Prince of Orange, the Stadtholder (hereditary ruler) of Holland.

In France, the young Prince Charles made quite an impression. He was 16 when he arrived in France and already six feet tall, with a dark complexion and dark black hair. Prince Charles had high hopes that his mother's influence with her nephew, Louis XIV, would persuade the French to give him the troops he needed to invade England and rescue his father. But the French court, dominated by Anne of Austria, regent for her young son, Louis XIV, and Cardinal Mazarin, her chief minister, refused to provide Charles with troops. The Prince soon departed for Holland where he hoped for more support from his sister and brother-in-law.

In the summer of 1648, there was a royalist uprising in England after the escape and arrest of King Charles I for the second time. Some of the ships of the English fleet declared for the King against Parliament and sailed off to the Netherlands. The nobles of Scotland were hostile to the Puritans and Parliament as well and had been courted by Charles I with promises of the king's favor if they helped to restore him. Prince Charles took command of the few royalist ships and attempted to blockade the Thames, but was soon forced to sail back to Holland for lack of supplies.

In January of 1649, Prince Charles learned that Parliament intended to put his father on trial for his life for high treasons. Charles, 19 years old, wrote a personal appeal to the leaders of Parliament, pleading for them to spare his father. With his letter, he sent a blank sheet of paper which he had signed and told them to write whatever conditions they wished from him in order to spare his father's life. He learned of his father's death a few weeks later, when his chaplain came to visit and addressed him as "Your Majesty."

When Parliament in England threatened to invade Holland and accused the Dutch of a deliberate insult by their support for Charles, the Dutch requested his departure. He joined his brother James and his mother in France in July of 1649.

Neither the French court nor the Spanish offered him any support. The Dutch dared not offend Cromwell's Protectorate. Charles was forced into an alliance with the leaders of the Scottish League and Covenant in Scotland. They were willing to accept and proclaim him as their king, but only if he signed the Covenant and pledged to impose Presbyterian government in Scotland, England, and Ireland and never to grant toleration to Catholics in any land he ruled. Charles made the pledge, though no one expected him to keep it, and sailed for Scotland – hoping to regain the throne of England with the help of a Scottish army. Cromwell responded by raising an army and marching on Edinburgh, and besieged the city. When a Scots army sallied out and gave battle, Cromwell's army decimated them and then occupied Edinburgh. Charles fled to the northwest. Charles spent the winter regrouping and rallying support among the highland nobles of Scotland. In 1651, with a newly raised (and poorly trained) army, he slipped past Edinburgh and marched into England, expecting to reclaim the throne of England. Charles led his forces south into England, and Cromwell took up the chase with his army from Edinburgh, leaving a small garrison behind under the command of General Monck.

Charles and his Cavalier officers had expected the countryside to rally to them and add to their numbers. They were bitterly disappointed when very few of the county militia bands appeared. Charles had badly miscalculated the loyalties of the Lancashire yeoman. Cromwell and the Parliamentary army finally caught up with Charles and his Cavalier and Scottish Highland forces at the English town of Worcester. On September 3, Cromwell attacked Charles's army and won an overwhelming victory.

Charles escaped with his bodyguard and fled into the countryside. Charles, 21 years old, was now a wanted man (Parliament offered a reward of £1,000 for his capture – the equivalent to $200,000 in 2009). Nonetheless, for the next six weeks, disguised at times as a servant, he managed to avoid detection and, with the help of royalist and catholic families, make his way through England to the Channel and escape by ship back to France where he rejoined his mother, Henrietta Maria, and his younger brother, James.

When the Protectorate under Cromwell went to war with the Dutch, Charles sought to take service in the Dutch Navy, but the French would not give him permission to leave. In 1654, the French negotiated a treaty with Cromwell. One of the conditions was that the French would no longer give Charles refuge. The Dutch had agreed to a similar condition in the treaty that ended their war. Charles left France, with a few friends, for a more austere exile in Cologne, Germany. In 1656, Charles and his small retinue of faithful followers moved to Bruges in the Spanish Netherlands (modern Belgium). He commanded his younger brother James to resign his commission in the French army and come and join him – which made James furious. He came to Bruges, but in a surly mood. Charles sent to France for his youngest brother Henry to come and join him as well. Charles had heard that his mother was attempted to persuade Henry to convert to Roman Catholicism and was both alarmed and displeased. The adoption of the Catholic religion by any of the three brothers would hurt Charles' chances of ever regaining the throne in England. In 1658, Charles and his little court moved to Brussels, still in the Spanish Netherlands, lying between France and Holland.

In September of 1658, Oliver Cromwell died and his son Richard was named as the new Protector. Charles debated with his advisors whether it was time to attempt another action with his small band of soldiers to try to win the crown of England on the field of battle. His advisors urged caution and so Charles waited. It was a wise decision. Richard had not served in Cromwell's army – which was the real source of political power in the Protectorate. The officers of the army distrusted him. When, after a few months, he called for the election of a new Parliament and began to implement the creation of an "other house" to balance the Commons, they rebelled. In April of 1659, the army demanded the dissolution of Richard's Parliament and the recall of the Rump Parliament – the Parliament whose members had originally been elected in 1640 (less the Presbyterian members who had been excluded by Pride's Purge of 1648). When the Rump Parliament reassembled, they made it clear they would not accept Richard as Protector either. When the Rump Parliament agreed to pay his debts and provide a pension, Richard agreed to resign his title of Protector on May 25, 1659. The Rump Parliament designated General Charles Fleetwood, Oliver Cromwell's son-in-law as the new commander-in-chief. Fleetwood was soon quarreling with the Rump Parliament as well, and in October, Parliament declared his commission void. The next day, Fleetwood expelled the Rump Parliament from their meeting hall in London. At this point, the Governor of Scotland, General George Monck, decided he had had enough. Monck had spent his life as a military officer, first in the army of King Charles I, then in the Parliamentary army. He had become a personal friend of Oliver Cromwell, who had appointed him first Governor of Ireland, and then Governor of Scotland. With General Fleetwood and the members of the Rump Parliament at odds and stalemated, General Monck led the soldiers under his command in an unopposed march on London. The soldiers in England, nominally under the command of General Fleetwood and General Lambert deserted their companies rather than fight the soldiers commanded by Monck. General Monck's army occupied London and took over the operations of the government. He then issued orders to reassemble the Parliament – not just the members of the Rump Parliament, but all of the members of the Long Parliament.

General Monck began a private correspondence with Charles II. In February of 1660, the reassembled Long Parliament, first elected in 1640, passed legislation calling for the election of a new Parliament and then voted to dissolve itself. The elections returned a large majority of MPs who favored the restoration of Charles II as the King of England. In April, Charles issued the Declaration of Breda, in which he guaranteed a free and general pardon to all of the enemies of his father and himself, excepting only those who had signed his father's death warrant in 1649. Charles further pledged to govern with the advice of Parliament,

and to refer to Parliament all disputes about contested grants and purchases of estates which had been made "in the distractions of so many years." He also promised to pay "all arrears due to the officers and soldiers of the army under the command of General Monck. On May 8th, 1660 the Convention Parliament declared that King Charles II had been the lawful monarch of England since his father's execution in January 1649. On the 25th of May, Charles (along with James and Henry) landed at Dover with much public celebration. He entered London on May 29th, 1660, his thirtieth birthday. In the end, he had regained his throne without the help of a single foreign soldier or the shedding of any English blood. His reversal of fortune was most unexpected and he and his advisors were the beneficiaries of both skill and luck.

Before the end of the year his joy at regaining his throne would be eclipsed by grief. In September, his youngest brother Henry died of smallpox just a few months after his 20th birthday. In December, his widowed sister Mary, 29, died of smallpox. Her husband, William II Prince of Orange had died of smallpox in 1650. Charles had been close to both Mary and Henry. Of the seven children born to Charles I and Henrietta Maria, only Charles II, James, and their youngest sister, Henrietta, who lived in Paris with their mother, were still alive.

Charles II kept his word and did not prosecute those who had fought against his father and served Cromwell during the eleven years of the protectorate. But his pardon did not extend to those who had participated in the trial and execution of his father. Of the 59 Commissioners who had signed Charles I's death warrant (called regicides by his son and by the Restoration Parliament), 39 were still alive in 1660. All were subject to a sentence of death; 13 were executed, 13 had their sentences commuted to life imprisonment, 11 fled abroad and later died in exile. Two died in prison awaiting trial.

The religious settlement proved more difficult. With the restoration of the monarchy, the bishops and priests of the Church of England wished to be restored to their position of unchallenged authority as well. The Presbyterians wished for a church patterned after the practices in Scotland. Charles detested the Presbyterians, but he was willing to grant them toleration – at least to preach and hold their own services – if toleration could also be extended the Catholics in England. The Catholic nobility had protected him and hidden him when he was a wanted man in 1651, trying to escape after the Battle of Worcester. They had been the most loyal supporters of his father. Parliament and the Bishops rejected the idea of religious toleration and instead enacted a series of laws called the Clarendon Code which required all officeholders at any level of government in England to be conforming members of the Church of

England and made the use of the Anglican Book of Common Prayer compulsory at all services. The code further prohibited any unlicensed (by the Bishop) religious assembly of more than five people and prohibited clergymen from coming within five miles of a parish from which they had been banished. Charles was disappointed, but could do little but go along. Two thousand clergymen (almost all of Presbyterian sympathies) resigned their parishes rather than conform to the Clarendon Code.

Charles' next obligation as king was to marry and insure an orderly succession to the throne. While in exile and without a crown, Charles had not been the most desirable of suitors. He had made overtures to several young women at the court in Paris, but none of them deemed him suitable for a marriage. He had already fathered one illegitimate child and had a well-earned reputation as a rogue. He had an open and scandalous relationship with Barbara Villiers Palmer which began in 1660 and continued throughout his reign. But he could not marry her because she already had a husband, she would bring no dowry, and the marriage would do nothing to advance the interests of England internationally. The dowry was Charles' most important consideration. He felt keenly the long years when he and his friends had suffered from poverty in exile. He remembered his father's difficulties caused by the necessity of seeking funds from Parliament. Negotiations with the Dutch, the French and the Spanish almost amounted to a bidding war as each offered Princesses with large dowries in the hopes of achieving an alliance with England. In the end, a marriage was agreed to with Princess Catherine, the daughter of the King of Portugal. She brought with her a large dowry in cash as well as the overseas territories of Tangier and Bombay, which became part of England's overseas empire.

Anne Hyde & James, Duke of York

There was another royal marriage in the first few years of Charles' reign as well. James announced his engagement to Anne Hyde, the daughter Sir Edward Hyde, Charles' chancellor, who had remained loyally in his service throughout his ten year exile. After the Restoration, Charles bestowed upon Sir Edward the title, Earl of Clarendon. The marriage was initially opposed by Charles and Sir Edward, but James insisted upon it, as Anne was already pregnant. Their first child, Charles, died in infancy as did several other children, but two daughters survived: Mary (born in 1662) and Anne (born in 1665).

In 1665, Charles faced the first crisis of his reign – an outbreak of the plague in London. From April of 1665 until February of 1666, several thousand died each week with the final toll reaching over 100,000. In June, the King and his family left the city for Oxford. Parliament relocated its sessions as well. Foul air was blamed for the outbreak and the authorities in London ordered the lighting of great bonfires, which were kept continually burning in hopes of cleansing the air. Residents of London were advised to smoke tobacco in order to ward off the plague. Not much seemed to help, but eventually the number of cases declined and the royal family and Parliament returned in the spring of 1666. In September of 1666 another disaster struck – fire broke out in the oldest part of London, the medieval quarter inside the old Roman city wall. In the tightly packed streets of wooden houses and thatched roofs it quickly flared out of control and spread. The fire burned for four days and destroyed over 10,000 houses and more than 80 churches, including St. Paul's Cathedral. The city authorities were slow to realize how dangerous the fire was and delayed creating firebreaks (which involved demolishing houses) to contain it. On the third day of the fire, Charles took personal charge and sent his brother James with a company of soldiers to organize efforts to contain the fire. James' experience serving in the French army and as Admiral of the Fleet stood him in good stead. He calmly organized a perimeter, conscripted men into teams of firefighters (mostly demolishing houses and creating a firebreak), and arranged for them to be paid and fed. James and a small company of cavalrymen rode from place to place along the edge of the fire and restored order. His actions made a lasting and favorable impression upon the citizens of London, who long remembered and told the tale of the long hours he worked to quench the fire.

After the fire was out, Charles took the unusual step of establishing a special Fire Court to resolve all disputes between tenants and landlords so that there would be no lingering legal disputes to delay rebuilding. It was also decreed that all new buildings must be constructed of brick and stone, rather than wood. Thatched roofs were outlawed. Charles also commissioned the greatest architect of the day, Sir Christopher Wren, to build fifty new churches to replace those which had been destroyed and to create a new St. Paul's. Wren designed a church in neo-classical, Renaissance style, very similar to the new St. Peter's which had been built in Rome, designed by Bramante and Michelangelo a hundred and fifty years before. It took ten years to design and thirty years to build, but the new St. Paul's began to host services in 1697, and was completed in 1708, in time for Wren's 76th birthday.

St. Paul's Cathedral
designed by Christopher Wren

Charles' foreign policy was dominated by relations with France and the Dutch. The Dutch had a vast global empire with trading stations located strategically around the world and a large merchant fleet which dominated world trade. The English merchant fleet was growing and competed with the Dutch merchants everywhere. Cromwell had fought the Dutch from 1652-1654 in a series of naval battles which established the superiority of the English navy and forced the Dutch to accept the English prohibition on conducting trade with its overseas colonies. In the 1660s, tensions rose again as the Dutch and the English competed for the right to conduct trade with overseas colonies. Parliament initially voted large subsidies to Charles to conduct a war against the Dutch. An English squadron was dispatched to the New World to seize the Dutch colony of New Amsterdam. The expedition was a success and the English renamed the settlement New York in honor of Charles' brother, James, Duke of York who was first Lord of the Admiralty. But England's initial successes were quickly reversed. The Dutch had learned their lessons from the war with Cromwell in the 1650s and had built larger ships with more guns. A series of naval battles were fought and won by the Dutch in the North Sea. The Dutch War dragged on. Charles ran short of money and much of his fleet had to return to harbor for lack of supplies. Sailors' pay was in arrears. By the third year of the war, in 1667, Parliament had grown weary and refused to grant further subsidies. In 1667, the Dutch fleet launched a raid on the English fleet, anchored in the Medway at the mouth of the river Thames. Fifteen English ships were destroyed and the flagship, HMS Royal Charles was captured and towed back to Holland. Charles had little choice but to negotiate for peace with the Dutch. The Dutch allowed the English to keep New York, but the English were forced to make concessions that allowed Dutch merchants to trade at English colonies around the world. Charles blamed Sir Edward Hyde (Lord Clarendon) for this humiliating defeat, and dismissed him as chancellor. Parliament, looking for someone to blame as well, passed a bill of impeachment for high treason against him. Hyde fled to France where he spent the last seven years of his life writing a history of the English Civil War from 1642-1651.

Charles remained short of money. Parliament stubbornly refused his requests to grant more. The nobles in Parliament were also increasingly concerned about Charles' religion. His marriage to a Catholic princess had not been popular. It reminded too many Englishmen of his father's marriage to the French Princess Henrietta Maria. Things were further complicated by the decision of James and his wife Anne to convert to Roman Catholicism in 1668. They continued to attend Anglican services, but rumors of their conversion were widespread.

Charles had lavished large amounts of money on his mistresses. He was desperate for money. In 1670, he negotiated a secret Treaty of Dover with his cousin, Louis XIV. Louis agreed to pay an annual subsidy to Charles each year. Charles agreed to support Louis in another war against the Dutch and to announce his conversion to Roman Catholicism "as soon of the welfare of the kingdom would permit." In 1672, Charles issued a Royal Declaration of Indulgence in which he announced the suspension of all penal laws against both Roman Catholics and non-conforming Protestant dissenters. In April, he joined the French in declaring war on the Dutch. A French army of 150,000 was dispatched by Louis to conquer the Dutch Provinces. The English fleet was to blockade the Dutch coast. Parliament opposed the Declaration of Indulgence, but initially supported the war with the Dutch, which Charles assured them would be over quickly.

The French army advanced to the Rhine, but once again, the Dutch Fleet won a large naval battle against the English in the North Sea. The Dutch then breached their dikes and flooded their fields making further advances by the French army impossible. Parliament lost patience with the war and refused further subsidies to Charles. They attacked his Royal Declaration of Indulgence and forced him to withdraw it. Charles was then forced to agree to a much stricter Test Act which required all public officials to denounce the Roman Catholic Church as "superstitious and idolatrous." Rather than take the oath, James resigned as Lord High Admiral, thus making public his conversion to Roman Catholicism.

James wife Anne had died in 1671. In 1673, he sought permission from Charles to marry Mary of Modena, a fifteen-year-old Italian princess, and devout Catholic. Charles attempted to persuade his brother to abandon the Catholic religion. He was opposed to the marriage. He finally agreed to it, only on condition that James' daughters, Mary and Anne, be placed with governesses and raised as Protestants.

By 1675, King Charles and Queen Catherine had been married for 14 years, but they had no children. All four of Queen Catherine's pregnancies had ended in miscarriages or stillbirths. Charles had fathered a dozen illegitimate children, but none of them could legally inherit the crown. His younger brother James was next in line for the throne, but James was now publically revealed to be a Roman Catholic. A movement began in Parliament to change the line of succession and to exclude James from ever becoming king. Charles remained loyal to his brother and opposed any exclusion act. He told Parliament that the order of succession was none of its business and could not be changed. He did agree, in 1677, that James' daughter Mary, then 15 and decidedly Protestant, should marry his nephew William III, Prince of Orange, and Stadholder of the Netherlands.

In 1678, the public pressure for an act excluding James from the line of succession erupted into a crisis. A rogue named Titus Oates made public accusations that there was a "Popish Plot" to assassinate the king and place James on the throne. Oates declared that he had overheard the plotters' plans for French and Spanish troops to occupy England and impose the Catholic Religion by force. Oates claimed to have converted to Catholicism and then reverted back to Anglicanism. While a Catholic in Paris, he said he had been part of a group of Jesuits charged by the Pope with bringing England forcibly back into the Catholic fold. Charles was skeptical and when Oates accused Queen Catherine of being part of the plot, Charles defended and protected her. But Parliament believed Oates and launched investigations and trials which led to the arrest and execution of 15 prominent Catholics. Charles had now completely lost the support of Parliament. When he dissolved it and called for new elections, things only got worse. The newly elected Parliament was even more hostile. Charles sent James and Mary to Scotland to reduce their public presence and prorogued Parliament repeatedly. When a newly-elected Parliament in 1681 took up an Exclusion Bill in its opening session, he dissolved it after only a few days. After 1681, Charles called no more Parliaments. Like his father and his cousin, Louis XIV, he resolved to govern and raise money without Parliament for as long as he could.

In 1683 a plot was uncovered by anti-Catholic Anglicans to murder Charles and James and place his illegitimate son, James Scott, the Duke of Monmouth, on the throne. The leaders were arrested and executed and Monmouth fled to the court of Charles' niece and nephew, William and Mary, in the Netherlands. James was invited to come back to London from Scotland and rejoin the Privy Council.

In February of 1685, Charles, age 55, suddenly collapsed, and died four days later. On his deathbed, he was received into the Roman Catholic Church. He was buried quietly in Westminster Abbey. His younger brother James was now King James III, and England had its first Catholic monarch since Henry VIII.

A new Parliament was assembled in May of 1685 and raised no objections to James' rule. In June, however he faced two co-ordinated rebellions, both launched from Holland. Archibald Campbell, the Earl of Argyll landed in Scotland and James Scott, Duke of Monmouth landed in Dorset, where he declared himself king. James was able to easily defeat both small forces and both Argyll and Monmouth were executed in July.

James proceeded to appoint a number of Catholic gentlemen to positions on his privy council and in the army and navy, claiming a "dispensing power" to waive the requirement of the Test Act in individual cases. When Parliament objected in November, James ordered them prorogued to an indefinite date, not to assemble again until he summoned them. Which he never did.

In 1686 James sought a court ruling upholding his power to dispense with the Test Act. He dismissed judges who dared to rule against him and eventually received the ruling he wanted. In 1687 he issued a Declaration for Liberty of Conscience in which he declared the suspension of the Test Act by virtue of the king's dispensing power, not just in individual cases, but in all cases. He ordered the Declaration to be read from the pulpits of every Anglican Church in England. When the Archbishop of Canterbury and six other bishops protested James' religious policies, he had them arrested and charged with sedition. On June 10 of 1688, James' second wife, Mary of Modena, after 15 years of marriage, gave birth to a son, whom the King named James Francis Edward. The leaders of Parliament, forbidden to meet for the previous three years, were now faced with a catholic monarch on the throne with a male heir, who would undoubtedly be raised a catholic. On June 30, seven Anglican nobles sent a letter to James' nephew, William III, Prince of Orange, and invited him to come to England with an army. Through the summer and fall, all England waited to see if William would respond and what James would do. Louis XIV offered James French troops for his defense, but James refused. On November 5th, William landed in Devon with an army of about 20,000 solders. He had sailed his fleet down the English Channel in full view of the garrison at Dover to demonstrate the size of his fleet. The landing site in Devon was chosen so that William's army would have time to make a slow, deliberate march back to the east towards London, giving time for those who might be wavering to make a decision to switch their allegiance from James to William.

James assembled his own troops in Salisbury, about halfway between Devon and London, but did not order them to attack. As William and his army advanced, some of James' officers deserted to William. On the 26th of November, James' received word that his daughter Anne had declared her allegiance to her brother-in-law and sister, William and Mary. On December 9th, Queen Mary of Modena and Prince James fled London for France. The next day, James attempted to flee by ship down the Thames. As he left, he tossed the Great Seal into the river. He was captured by English fisherman and returned to London. William sent word to James that he could not guarantee the King's safety and suggesting that he should depart London. William gave orders to his Dutch troops that they should not prevent James from leaving, but should let him slip through. On December 23, James set sail across the English Channel to France, where he joined his wife and six-month-old son at the court of Louis XIV.

In 1689, James landed in Ireland with troops loaned to him by Louis XIV. The Irish Parliament proclaimed their allegiance to him and adopted an act granting religious freed to both Catholics and Protestants in Ireland. For a year, James ruled in Dublin and made plans to win back his crown in England. In 1690, William crossed the Irish Sea and led an army of English and Dutch soldiers toward Dublin. At the Battle of the Boyne River, William's army defeated James, though James was able to retire to Dublin in good order. Again though, James lost his nerve. When William's army approached Dublin, he gave orders for a retreat to Limerick and then abandoned Ireland and returned to France.

James spent his last eleven years living at a Chateau in France provided to him by Louis XIV, still maintaining that he was the rightful King of England. He died in 1701. In 1702, James' younger daughter Anne succeeded to the throne when William died. After Anne died (in 1714), her younger half-brother, James Edward Francis (James III to his supporters) led a rebellion in Scotland claiming to be the rightful King of England and Scotland. The rebellion of 1715 lasted only a few months. In 1745, James' grandson, Charles Edward Stuart led a second rebellion in Scotland which was also defeated. Many Scottish veterans of the '15 and the '45 emigrated to the colonies in North America to escape retribution for their part in the two rebellions.

Jan Sobieski

Born 1629, King of Poland 1674-1696

The Poles first appeared in history in the fifth century under the name of Poliani. There is a record of the King of Poland converting to Christianity in 966 AD. But the country did not rise into much prominence until the fourteenth century; and it attained its greatest splendor in the seventeenth.

The name Poland is derived from a word meaning plains. For many centuries great herds of cattle, horses, and swine have been raised within its territory; and cereals, hemp, timber, honey, and wax have been produced in large quantities. It was a prosperous, wealthy territory, with many advantages and natural resources.

Jan Sobieski was born in 1629 to a family that was already famous. His father ruled one of the regions of Poland and was Castellan (governor or commander) of the castle in Krakow, one of the chief Polish cities. Jan grew up in Krakow and undoubtedly learned much from his father about the military sciences. But Krakow was also famous for its University, which had been founded in 1364, second only in prestige in central Europe to the great University in Prague. Jan enrolled at the University and completed his degree in 1647. His father now arranged for Jan and his younger brother, Marek, to make a grand tour of Europe. The two brothers traveled through Germany, the Netherlands, and France where they met and were befriended by William II of Orange, Charles II, the exiled King of England, and the great French general, Louis II de Bourbon (also known as Le Grand Condé). Jan showed a gift for languages and was equally at home in French, German, Italian, and Latin.

When Jan and Marek Sobieski returned to Poland in 1648, they learned that their father had been killed in battle against Russian Cossacks. Jan and Marek enlisted in the Polish army as junior officers. In their first battle, they fought bravely with the cavalry, but Marek was taken prisoner and died. Jan was rewarded with promotion and given command of his own company of cavalry. The Cossack rebellion ended with a week-long battle at Berestechko in 1651 where the Polish cavalry defeated the Cossacks, despite being outnumbered almost 2:1. The Polish King, John Casimir, took notice of the young officer, Jan Sobieski, and sent him as an envoy to the Turkish capital of Istanbul the following year. Jan studied the Turkish military organization and tactics closely, and learned their language.

In 1654, Russia attacked Poland, and in 1655, Sweden invaded from the north. Sweden nearly succeeded in conquering all of Poland, but the Polish army rallied and after three years of heavy, devastating fighting, managed to defeat the Swedes and forced them to withdraw. Jan Sobieski again distinguished himself and was promoted to general. At the end of the war, the King named him Grand Hetman of the Crown, or commander-in-chief of the entire Polish army. In 1665, Jan married the French princess, Marie Casimire Louise de la Grange d'Arquien.

In the 17th century, the Turks were at the height of their power in southeastern Europe. For centuries, they had campaigned from Istanbul north and west through the Balkans, up the Danube River valley towards Hungary and Austria. Their flag had waved over the important Danube River city of Belgrade a hundred and fifty years, and Belgrade was the gateway to Hungary.

The Turkish fleets swept the Mediterranean. They had captured the island of Crete from the powerful state of Venice; and they had fortified the Dardanelles, so that no ships could enter the Black Sea without their permission.

Because the territory of Poland was famous for its wheat and cattle, the Turks greatly desired to possess it. In 1672, they invaded Poland with a large army; but the Poles met them bravely and in a great battle in which Jan Sobieski served as commander-in-chief, the Polish forces defeated the Turks and forced them to retreat.

Shortly after, King John Casimir died quite suddenly; and the Diet assembled to select a successor. Jan Sobieski entered the hall where the Diet was in session and nominated a French prince. Then one of the nobles was heard to say, "Let a Pole rule Poland." Sobieski was at once proposed and elected with hardly a dissenting voice.

As they had done in 1529, the Turks gathered a vast army and marched against Vienna in 1683. Vienna was not only the principal city of Austria, but the capital of the German Empire, ruled by Leopold I. Though Leopold wore the crown of Charlemagne, he was not worthy to do so. As soon as he heard that the Turks were marching toward Vienna he fled from the city. Many of the nobles and wealthy people followed his example.

Count Starhemberg who was in command of the garrison stayed at his post, and did everything possible to prepare the city for the approaching Turkish army. There was much to be done. The fortifications needed repair and there was very little time and many had fled. Those who remained, both men and women, all aided in the work. The women mixed mortar and carried stone while the men built up the walls.

One day, as the people of Vienna were looking eastward, they saw columns of smoke on the horizon. Crops were burning, and houses and villages were in flames. This told them, only too plainly, that the Turks were approaching. At sunrise, on the fourteenth of July, 1683, the Turkish army appeared before the city walls. Their camp made a semicircle or crescent reaching more than halfway around the city.

Living conditions in Vienna became difficult. Thousands from the countryside had sought refuge in the city. There was not enough food. Conditions were unsanitary. As in Athens, during the terrible siege by the Spartans in the Peloponnesian War, so now in Vienna the plague broke out. Thousands died. Then a fire broke out. A great many houses were burned, and hundreds of families were rendered homeless. It looked as though Vienna would soon fall to the Turks. But then help arrived unexpectedly. A large Polish army was spotted approaching the city.

As soon as he had heard of the Turkish threat to Vienna, King Jan Sobieski of Poland had set out to relieve the beleaguered city. He had sixty-five thousand men in his army; and John George, the Elector of Saxony had joined him with thirteen thousand more. As they approached the city, they prepared to attack the Turkish army.

The Turkish General, Kara Mustafa, now faced a terrible choice. He had to divide his forces – part to continue the siege of the city, and part to face the Poles and Germans who were preparing to attack.

Before beginning the attack on the Turks, Sobieski made a speech to his men in which he said, "Not Vienna alone, but Christendom looks to you to-day. Not for an earthly sovereign do you fight. You are soldiers of the King of kings."

The army then raised a cry of "Sobieski! Sobieski!" The name Sobieski was well known to the Turks, for they had met him before, and thousands of Turks fled before hundreds of his Poles. His very name seemed to fill them with dread. Large numbers of the Turkish soldiers stood their ground, and fought desperately; but they could not withstand the furious charges of the Poles.

Sobieski himself went into the battle singing the words of the psalm beginning: "Not unto us, O Lord, not unto us, but unto thy name give glory, for thy mercy, and for thy truth's sake." Six of the sultan's pashas, or generals, were killed; and the grand vizier, or prime minister of Turkey, abandoned his splendid green silk tent that was embroidered with gold and silver, and fled for his life.

The whole Moslem army was routed; and Jan Sobieski and his troops entered the city in triumph. A great service of thanksgiving was held in the cathedral; and one of the priests preached a sermon from the text: "There was a man sent from God whose name was John."

Never again did the Turks attack Vienna. Over the next hundred years, city after city was lost to their empire; and all Hungary was finally won back from them. After Sobieski's great victory, the power of the Turks steadily waned. They were slowly pushed to the eastward until their only foothold in Europe was the city of Constantinople, which they call Istanbul.

The reign of Jan Sobieski was the most brilliant in Polish history. But the constant dissensions and the unending turbulence of the Polish nobles frustrated all his efforts to strengthen the kingdom, and prepared the way for its final dismemberment and ruin within a century of his death.

In 1683 the Polish astronomer, Johannes Hevelius, named a gleaming expanse of star dust in the brightest part of the Milky Way "Scutum Sobiescianum" or "Sobieski's Shield." It is the only constellation that is not named for a figure from the ancient classical world. Nowadays, the name has been shortened to Scutum, but until the stars forget to shine, or men to watch them, the name of the great Polish hero, Jan Sobieski, who altered the course of history by defeating the Turkish army at Vienna, will never be forgotten.

William of Orange

Born 1650, King of England 1688 – 1702

William was born in Holland in 1650. He was prince of the distinguished house of Orange, which for many years had been prominent in the history of the Netherlands. His father, William II died eight days before he was born from smallpox. He was thus the Prince of Orange from the moment of his birth. His mother, Mary Stuart, was younger sister to King Charles II of England. She died of smallpox when he was ten years old.

William was carefully educated. One of his tutors was Constantijn Huygens, who had been secretary to both Prince Frederick and Prince William II (and was one of the early patrons of Rembrandt). From 1659 to 1666, William's tutors had him spend much of his time at the University of Leiden, though he was never enrolled as a student.

After the death of his father, the Parliament (States-General) of the United Provinces suspended the office of Stadtholder (or Head of State) and left it vacant. When William turned 18, he was admitted to the ruling council of the Dutch provinces, but the leading politicians refused to grant him the title of Stadtholder. In 1670, William traveled to England to negotiate on behalf of the United Provinces with his uncle, King Charles II. King Charles liked his nephew, then twenty years old, but he remained an ally of King Louis XIV. When the French King invaded the Netherlands, with the support of the English fleet in 1672, the Estates General appointed William as Stadtholder and placed him in command of all Dutch forces, though he was only twenty-two.

King Louis XIV had dispatched an army of one hundred and twenty-five thousand men, under the command of Turenne and Condé, to conquer the Netherlands. England sent her fleet to crush the power of the Dutch. Town after town was taken by the French, and the Dutch were in a terrible plight.

Young as he was, William carried on the war like an experienced general. His army had reverses at first; but his belief in the final triumph of the Dutch never left him.

Once a despondent official said to him, "Do you not see that the country is lost?"

"Lost!" replied William, "No, it is not lost; and I shall never see it lost!"

In this spirit of confidence he fought his enemies, never despairing, never acknowledging defeat. After many successes the French were about to seize the city of Amsterdam. William ordered the dikes to be cut, and the waters of the North Sea spread over the lowlands. The growing crops were ruined, but the flood checked the invading army.

In 1674, peace was made with England, and France, though France had inflicted great disasters upon the Netherlands and occupied part of her territory. But Louis was forced to withdraw from the country. The Dutch, under the heroic leadership of their young Stadtholder, maintained their independence.

Mary Stuart,
daughter of James, Duke of York

In 1677, William sought the hand of King Charles II's niece, Mary, the fifteen-year-old daughter of Charles' younger brother James, the Duke of York. Charles and William both favored the match, believing that it would strengthen an alliance between England and Holland, and help to deter the ambitions of the French King Louis XIV. James initially opposed the marriage, but eventually gave his consent, hoping that the marriage of his daughter to the Protestant leader of the Netherlands would improve his popularity with the English people.

In 1685, on the death of King Charles II, the Duke of York came to the English throne as King James II. He quickly aroused great dissatisfaction in England by his appointment of Roman Catholics to key offices and his dissolution of Parliament. When his second wife gave birth to a son in June of 1688, a letter was sent to William of Orange, inviting him and his wife Mary, to become joint sovereigns of England.

This letter was signed by seven leading men of both the great political parties in England. It assured William that it was the universal wish of the English nation that he should become its ruler. William accepted the invitation. The Netherlands, glad to have their honored Stadtholder on the English throne, furnished him with an army of about thirteen thousand men, and a fleet of more than six hundred ships, and with these forces he reached England in November, 1688.

William landed his army in Exeter, and began marching towards London. The English people welcomed him enthusiastically. Thousands of the nobles, gentry and common people flocked to his standard. His army rapidly increased. Everywhere in England there was great rejoicing at his arrival.

King James gathered a strong force, mostly from Scotland and Ireland, and marched to Salisbury to check the revolt. But William continued his march toward London, and the king's army fell back in disorder. Many of the officers and men deserted. James gave up the struggle in despair, and hastened to London. There he learned that his daughter, Anne (Mary's sister), had left his palace to join Prince William.

"God help me," cried the king, "for my own children have forsaken me!"

His spirit was broken, and he prepared for a rapid journey to France. He knew that the throne was lost to him. He resolved to flee from England and cast himself upon the hospitality of his cousin, the French king, Louis XIV.

Leaving the palace at night, and in disguise, he threw the seals of state into the Thames, and then took a boat to a ship which was lying some distance down the river. James hoped to sail in this ship to France; but his escape was prevented by a fisherman who thought him a suspicious character, and he was brought back to London. William then dispatched a letter to James (his father-in-law and uncle) informing him and that he could not guarantee his safety and suggesting that he should withdraw from London. William then gave orders to his troops that James should be allowed to leave England if he wished, and Dutch officers escorted James to the coast, where he sailed across the channel to France.

William and Mary, with the army that supported them, now arrived in London. They were greeted with acclamation. A committee of Parliament drew up a Declaration of Rights, which was presented to William and Mary. It declared what the rights of Englishmen are, stated that no sovereign could interfere with those rights, and expressed the resolve of both houses of Parliament to maintain them.

The Declaration of Rights was a second Magna Charta. William and Mary both signed it, and they were then, in February, 1689, declared king and queen of England. This change in the rulers—the abdication of King James and the coming of William and Mary—is called the Glorious Revolution by English historians.

The Revolution was easily accomplished in England; but in Ireland there was decided opposition to it. Londonderry and Enniskillen were the only Irish towns that declared for William and Mary. The other towns were strongly in favor of James. In 1689, James sailed from France to Ireland with troops loaned to him by the King of France. Once in Ireland he collected an army and began a war on those who supported the new sovereigns. Those who fought for James were called "Jacobites" and those who supported William were called "Orangemen." The war in Ireland lasted but a few months. At the battle of the Boyne, on July 12, 1690, James's army was defeated, and all resistance in Ireland came to an end. James fled Ireland and returned to France.

William was now formally recognized as king of England, Scotland, and Ireland.

Louis XIV's assistance to James was treated as an act of war by the English Parliament. Louis now resumed his campaign to conquer the Netherlands. It was necessary for William to visit the European continent each year to command his forces in the field. He would leave England in the spring and return in the fall. While he was absent from England, Mary ruled the kingdom, and ruled it well.

William was engaged for some years in the contest on the continent. He won many great battles, but he also suffered disastrous defeats. While he was in Europe another attempt was made by James to invade England and regain the throne.

In 1692, Louis XIV again provided James with soldiers and war ships; and an expedition sailed for England. James was confident of success; and all associated with him thought it would be an easy matter to accomplish the undertaking. Near the coast of Normandy the invading fleet came upon the combined English and Dutch fleet. Off Cape La Hogue, a furious battle took place. The English and Dutch gained a brilliant victory. James sailed back to France, and never again made a movement to recover the English throne.

While England and France were fighting in Europe, the colonies of the two countries were fighting in America. The war is known in American history as King William's War.

William and Mary had no children. When Mary died in 1694 of smallpox, William was deeply grieved. From 1694 to his death, he ruled as the sole sovereign. In 1701, with William's agreement, Parliament passed an Act of Settlement which provided that Mary's younger sister Anne would succeed to the throne, and following her, the heirs of Sophia, the Electress of Hannover. In 1702, William was out riding when his horse stumbled, causing him to fall and break his collarbone. He died four weeks later of pneumonia, at the age of 52.

The reign of William and Mary was of great significance to the English colonies in North America which eventually became the United States. Those sovereigns were not accepted by the people of England until they had signed the Declaration of Rights; and the very first Act passed by Parliament during their reign was one which made the Declaration a part of the laws of the land.

That Declaration secured their rights not only to the subjects who lived in the "mother country," but also to those in the colonies. One of its provisions was "that it is the right of the subjects to petition the king."

When a later King of England, George III, spurned the petitions of the colonists, and otherwise violated the rights claimed in the Declaration, just as James II had done, the colonists branded him as a tyrant. The American colonists maintained, therefore, when they fought the battles of the American Revolution, that they were acting as the people of England had done a hundred years before, when they dethroned James and offered the crown to William and Mary. There is thus a very close connection between the English Revolution of 1688 (often called the Glorious Revolution), and the American Revolution of 1775-1783.

John Locke

1632-1704

John Locke's family were Puritans. His father, John Sr., was an attorney and court clerk for several justices in Bristol, a port city in the west of England. He fought in the English Civil War with the Parliamentary army as a cavalry officer. John Jr. was born in a small village just outside of Bristol. When he was fifteen, his parents sent him to London to attend the prestigious Westminster School. He was a seventeen-year-old student in London when King Charles I was tried and executed. In 1652, he enrolled at Oxford University. He received a bachelor's degree in 1656, a master's degree in 1658. After completing his degrees, Locke was given a fellowship to continue his studies at Oxford. He also took on the task of serving as a tutor to the next generation of undergraduates. He continued his studies of medicine and opened a practice as a physician. Years later, in 1674, Oxford conferred upon him a degree of bachelor of medicine.

In 1660, Locke's father died and he inherited a small estate which allowed him to make his living arrangements in Oxford a little more comfortable. Locke's mother must have died sometime before this, but we do not know what year. As he continued his life as a scholar in Oxford, Locke received appointments to deliver lectures on Greek grammar, in the arts of rhetoric, and on moral philosophy – all standard parts of the Oxford curriculum. If he took any notice of the great events connected with the restoration of King Charles II, there is no record of it. He was a twenty-seven year old Oxford scholar and tutor at the time, and seems not to have been passionate about politics.

In 1666, Anthony Cooper, the 1st Earl of Shaftesbury went to Oxford seeking treatment for an illness. He was treated by an earnest and intelligent young man, then conducting medical research in Oxford named John Locke. Shaftesbury was not only grateful for the wise medical advice, but found John Locke to be extremely well read and quite knowledgeable in matters of politics and philosophy. Shaftesbury persuaded Locke, then 34, to return with him to London and serve as his household physician, as well as personal secretary.

After the disastrous Dutch War and the fall and exile of King Charles II's chancellor, Edward Hyde, Shaftesbury became a prominent member of the King's council. In 1672, King Charles appointed Shaftesbury as his Lord Chancellor. Shaftesbury quarreled increasingly with Charles over the succession issues. After a year, Charles replaced him as chancellor, and Shaftesbury withdrew from the King's council and for a time kept a much lower political profile.

From 1675-1679, John Locke lived abroad, in France. He travelled first to Paris, and then made an extended stay in Montpellier in southern France of almost a year. In 1677, Locke returned to Paris. In both Paris and Montpellier, Locke spent his time reading, writing, and on occasion studying medicine and comparing notes with local physicians.

In England, Shaftesbury found himself so far out of King Charles' favor that he was accused of treason and confined under arrest to the Tower of London for a year before the King ordered the charges dismissed and had him released. In 1679, the King once again appointed Shaftesbury to his privy council, but Shaftesbury remained opposed to the King over the matter of succession. When Shaftesbury rejoined the King's Privy Council, Locke returned to England from France and resumed his duties as Shaftesbury's personal secretary and physician.

Shaftesbury devoted himself increasingly to the cause of passing the Exclusion Bill which would have barred King Charles' younger brother James from the succession because he was a Roman Catholic. In 1681, Charles dissolved Parliament as it was about to take up the Exclusion Bill. Shaftesbury was implicated in a Protestant plot against Charles and fled to the Netherlands. John Locke, age 51, went with him, along with the Duke of Monmouth, Charles' illegitimate son.

Shaftesbury died in exile in the Netherlands in 1683. Shaftesbury left a small annuity for the benefit of John Locke, his longtime secretary and physician, and Locke was able to live in pleasant circumstances in Amsterdam. He toured the provinces of the Netherlands, visited the medical faculty of the University of Leiden and was consulted from time to time on questions of medicine by Dutch physicians.

At some point during his exile, he was introduced to the young Prince William of Orange and his English wife, Mary, daughter of King James II, who befriended him and made him an honored guest at their court.

In 1688, after five years in exile, Locke returned to England with Queen Mary to join King William III who had just been recognized as King of England by Parliament when James II fled to France. King William and Queen Mary were anxious to honor their friend, John Locke, the Oxford physician. They offered to appoint him to a post as ambassador to either Prussia or Austria, but he wrote them that he must decline the honor due to his poor health. Finally, they persuaded him to accept appointment as a commissioner of appeals in the office of Exchequer, where he might be called upon to rule upon the validity of claims for payment against the crown. Locke took no active part in politics or the Parliaments which met after the Glorious Revolution of 1688, but he did have a number of friends and a few former pupils from Oxford who became MPs.

In 1689, he published an essay titled **A Letter Concerning Toleration** and shortly thereafter a lengthier piece titled **Two Treatises of Government**. In 1690, he published **An Essay Concerning Human Understanding**. He had begun working on these essays many years earlier and had re-written and polished them many times. They were not used by those the Parliamentary leaders who led the Glorious Revolution, but they reflected many of the ideas which were current in England at the time.

Locke's argument in **Concerning Toleration** is that all Protestant religious groups should be granted the freedom to meet, preach, and worship as they chose, undisturbed. He rejected toleration for Roman Catholics, because their religion required obedience to a foreign power, the Pope. He pronounced atheists as not worthy of toleration either since they would have no fear of future divine punishment for violating their promises, covenants, and oaths.

In **Two Treatises of Government**, Locke first attacks the "false principles and foundation of Sir Robert Filmer" who had defended the divine right of kings. In the second essay he discusses the "true origin, extent, and end of Civil Government." Locke is the first political philosopher to describe all men as "created equal" and endowed by God with certain inalienable rights. Locke enumerates the fundamental rights granted to an individual by God as the "right to life," the "right to liberty," and the "right to property." He then asserts that the only legitimate authority for government is the consent of the governed given in a social compact, and states that the purpose of government is to protect the rights given to an individual by God from being encroached upon by all others. The ideas in the **Two Treatises** gave a philosophical justification for the overthrow of James II and the establishment of a new "social contract" with King William and Queen Mary by Parliament. Locke's essays were widely read in the century following his death and many of his ideas are repeated in the Declaration of Independence and the US Constitution. Samuel Adams of Boston quoted Locke frequently in his writings. Thomas Jefferson stated that John Locke was one of the three greatest men who had ever lived.

In Locke's **Essay Concerning Human Understanding**, he argues that every newborn is born with a blank slate (tabula rasa) and that all knowledge, concepts, and ideas are acquired through the senses, with sensations acted upon, analyzed, and synthesized by reason. He dismisses the idea that there are any innate ideas or principles.

Locke was now 58 years old, and his health was not good. He was subject to frequent fits of violent coughing – what we would now call asthma. The air in London made his condition worse, and so he accepted an invitation to join the household of Sir Francis and Lady Masham at their estate in Oates Manor, about twenty-five miles north of London and far enough into the country to enjoy better air. He kept up a considerable correspondence with a wide variety of correspondents and enjoyed visits from, among others, Isaac Newton, who like Locke was a member of the Royal Society for the Improvement of Natural Knowledge, which had been founded in 1660. Locke used his influence and friendship with the King and Queen to assist Newton in obtaining appointment to a professorship at Cambridge University.

In 1696, Locke was persuaded to accept appointment by the King to a newly formed "commission for promoting the trade of the kingdom, and for inspecting and improving the plantations in America and elsewhere." Locke was one of eight commissioners, but he quickly became the leader of the commission. He worked diligently at this task, which involved collecting information from all of England's dominions, interviewing witnesses and making recommendations to King and Parliament.

Locke's difficulties in breathing grew worse due to his extended stays in London on commission business. In 1700, he resigned from his position on the commission and returned to more or less permanent retirement in the country with the Masham's at Oates Manor. He was now 68 years old. He resumed both his correspondence and his writing and revising. He was saddened in 1702, to hear of the death of his friend, King William II.

In 1704, at the age of 72, John Locke died peacefully in the country at Oates Manor. After his death, Lady Masham described him this way:

> "He was always, in the greatest and in the smallest affairs of human life, as well as in the speculative opinions, disposed to follow reason, whosoever it were that suggested it; he being ever a faithful servant to Truth; never abandoning her for anything else, and following her, and for her own sake, purely."

Johan Pachelbel

1653-1706

St. Sebaldus Church
in Nuremberg,
where Pachelbel was organist

Johann Pachelbel was born in Nuremberg, Germany on September 1st, 1653. Nuremberg had long been a prominent city in the German Empire and had adopted Lutheranism early in the Reformation. It suffered terribly in the Thirty Years War, especially in 1632, when a Swedish-German army under Gustavus Adolphus was besieged for eleven weeks by the Catholic forces led by Wallenstein. During the siege 10,000 residents, or a quarter of the city's population died. Up until that time Nuremberg had been a prosperous city of 40,000 in 1600. By 1650, it had declined to 25,000 and did not recover for two centuries.

Pachelbel was a bright child who excelled at school. He was offered a place at the academically elite gymnasium (German high school) which had been founded by Luther and Melanchthon. In 1669 he completed his studies there and entered the University in Nuremberg. In addition to his academic abilities, he demonstrated a remarkable aptitude for music. He had an excellent voice and received music lessons from Heinrich Schwemmer, the choir director at the St. Sebaldus Church in Nuremberg. By the time he was sixteen, he was also playing the organ.

Pachelbel's father, a wine merchant of modest means was unable to finance his university studies, and so Pachelbel left Nuremberg for Regensburg in 1670. He was given an academic scholarship at the university. While pursuing his studies, he also continued his music lessons - receiving private instruction from the organist, Kaspar Prentz.

Three years later, at the age of twenty, Pachelbel accepted a position as deputy organist at St. Stephen's Cathedral in Vienna. Vienna, on the Danube, was the capital of the Habsburg

Empire. The Habsburg court attracted musicians and artists from all over Europe. The court musicians included a number of composers and performers from Italy, whose style was quite different from the northern, Lutheran traditions that Pachelbel had grown up with in Nuremberg. Pachelbel's style became a blend of both.

In 1677, Pachelbel, now 24, moved back to central Germany, taking a position as court organist for the Duke of Saxe-Eisenach. In Eisenach, he was befriended by the musical family of Johann Ambrosius Bach (1645-1695), whose three brothers were all court musicians. Pachelbel was employed as a tutor for Johann Ambrosius Bach's oldest son, Johann Christoph Bach III, who was six. After only a year, Pachelbel was called away from Eisenach to a more prestigious position at the nearby city of Erfurt, as organist at the Predigerkirche, or "Preachers' Church." Here he established a reputation as an outstanding composer and organist. While in Erfurt, Pachelbel rented his house from Johann Christian Bach, who was a cousin of Johann Ambrosius Bach.

In 1681, Pachelbel, now 28 married Barbara Gabler, and two years later became the father of son. Unfortunately both wife and son died during an outbreak of the plague. Pachelbel composed a chorale that year titled "Musical Thoughts on Death."

Three years later, Johann married Judith Trommer. Johann and Judith had seven children, five sons and two daughters.

In 1690, after twelve years in Erfurt, Johann decided it was time to move on. He worked for two years in Stuttgart, and then for two years in Gotha. He remained good friends with the Bach family. In 1694, his former pupil, Johann Christoph Bach married and his friend Johann Ambrosius invited him to compose some appropriate music and perform for the wedding. At the wedding, Pachelbel was undoubtedly introduced to Johann Ambrosius' eleventh and youngest child, nine-year-old Johann Sebastian Bach.

In 1695, Pachelbel came full circle and was offered and accepted the position of organist at the St. Sebaldus Church in his hometown of Nuremberg. By now he was a famous and accomplished composer and the town fathers were anxious for him to return to the city of his birth. They made him a generous offer, which he quickly accepted.

From 1695 until his death in 1706, Pachelbel spent his days playing the organ at St. Sebaldus, composing new chamber music, chorales, and organ pieces, and enjoying his family. Two of his children followed their father's footsteps and became organ composers as well. One of them, Wilhelm Hieronymus Pachelbel succeeded his father as organist at St. Sebaldus.

Another of his sons, Charles Theodore Pachelbel, moved to London for a time before emigrating, in 1733, to the English colony of Massachusetts. He quickly became the organist at Trinity Church in Newport, Rhode Island. In 1736, he gave two public concerts in New York City. After seven years in Rhode Island, he became the organist at St. Phillip's Church in Charleston, South Carolina. He held that position until his death in 1750, at the age of sixty.

Approximately 530 musical compositions have been attributed to Pachelbel including : 100 choral preludes, several hundred fugues; and about a dozen works of chamber music. His most famous composition is a piece of chamber music called the Canon in D major, written for three violins, a bass continuo and gigue violin. It is now one of the most famous and recognized baroque compositions. It was written early in Pachelbel's career, about 1680 – when he would have been 27 or 28 years old. Although it was certainly performed by Pachelbel in the cities where he was employed, the manuscript was never published. It was only discovered and published first in 1920 and became famous in the 1970s.

And the nine-year-old Johann Sebastian Bach? He certainly would have known all about Johan Pachelbel. Johann Sebastian was tutored in music by his eldest brother, Johann Christoph, who in turn, had been Johan Pachelbel's student. But Johann Sebastian Bach's story will be told in Famous Men of the 18th Century.

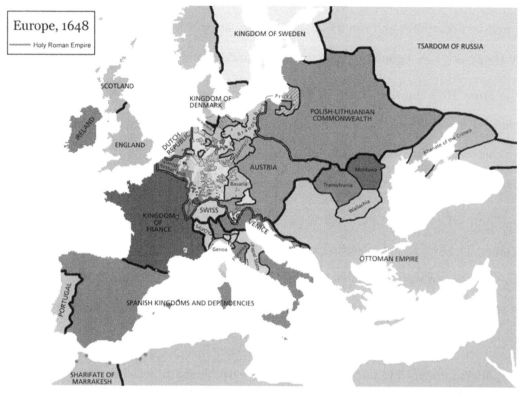

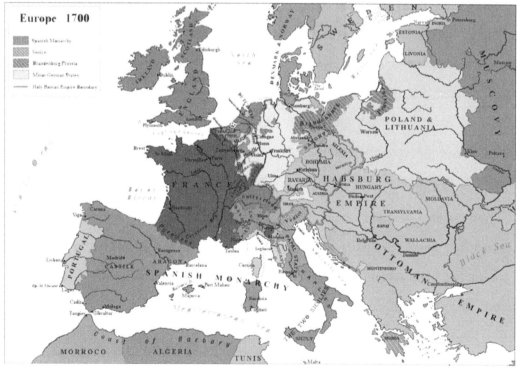

Louis XIV

1638-1715

After the death of Richelieu, in 1642, Louis XIII, king of France, followed the advice of his great prime minister and called Cardinal Mazarin to fill his place. But Louis XIII lived only six months after Richelieu passed away. He died in 1643, and his son Louis XIV succeeded him as king.

Louis XIV had the longest and most brilliant reign in the history of France. His reign of seventy-two years is the longest ever for the monarch of any European country. The French people have always called him "The Grand Monarch." He was born in 1638, and became king when he was but five years old. His mother, Anne of Austria, governed the kingdom, as regent, until he was thirteen; but Mazarin was retained in office, and quickly became the real ruler of France.

Mazarin was a great statesman, but he was determined to have his own way. Many of the things he did cost a great deal of money; and so he made the people of France pay very heavy taxes, and this caused them to dislike him exceedingly. Finally they became so discontented that, in 1648, the people of Paris (and later much of the rest of France) began a revolt. This revolt was known as the War of the Fronde, which means the War of the Sling. The name was given to ridicule the revolting party who were dismissed as chiefly peasants who were too poor to buy proper arms. They were compared to the disorderly boys of Paris who sometimes fought with slings. In fact, the rebellion included members of the legislative council of Paris, as well as many of the nobles, including Louis' uncle Gaston, the Duke of Orleans.

The rebellion lasted four years, and at its close Anne of Austria was forced to dismiss Mazarin who went into exile. The exile was only temporary, however, for within six months, Mazarin returned with an army, intent on freeing Anne from the princes of France who had received seats on the council of regency and were her rivals for influence over her young son. The Prince of Condé raised an army to oppose Mazarin, but Marshal Turenne, a veteran commander of French troops in the final phase of the Thirty Years' War, remained loyal to Anne and joined his army to Mazarin's. After a year of maneuver and fighting, Turenne was able to decisively defeat Condé and peace was restored to France.

As a boy Louis XIV had been more fond of military exercises than of study. He took great delight in handling swords and beating drums. The boys belonging to some of the noble families of France were the playmates of the young king. He formed them into a company of soldiers, and spent some time every day in drilling them.

In 1651, when he reached the age of thirteen, he resolved to begin ruling in his own name. He declared his independence from his mother, but retained Cardinal Mazarin as his chief minister. His first act as king in his own name was to join the army of General Turenne in the field.

RECEPTION OF TURENNE BY LOUIS XIV AT VERSAILLES.

Louis went with General Turenne into the South of France upon a military expedition against the forces of the Prince of Condé. He was greatly pleased with life in the army and came back to Paris enthusiastic about military tactics.

"General Turenne," said the young king, "when I make war you must lead my troops."

"I deeply thank you, Sire, for your good opinion of me," replied the famous general. "I should be glad indeed to have command of Your Majesty's army in any war in which you may be engaged."

"Well, general," said Louis, "I feel sure that I shall have lots of wars; and you must be ready to help me."

Years afterwards Louis's words came true. He carried on many wars. In some of them Turenne won fame as one of the greatest commanders of his time.

Louis saw that Mazarin was managing the affairs of the nation with great skill; so he allowed him to do as he thought best, while His Majesty devoted himself to a life of pleasure.

But in 1661, when Louis was twenty-three, Mazarin died. The day after Mazarin's death the officers of the government assembled at the palace, all eager to know which of them was to be the new prime minister.

"To whom shall we speak in the future about the business of the kingdom?" asked one of them.

"To me," answered the king. "Hereafter I shall be my own prime minister."

After thus taking matters into his own hands he reigned for more than fifty years. He placed in control of the different departments of the government the best men he could find; and one of his officers, the famous Jean-Baptiste Colbert, managed the money matters of the kingdom in such a manner as to make his name illustrious for all time. He made the taxes less burdensome to the people. At the same time, he so fostered the industries of the kingdom that the revenue was greatly increased.

Louis improved the condition of the French people. He encouraged manufacturers. He even established some factories at the expense of the government; so that, during his reign, France became famous for her woolens and carpets, her silks and tapestries.

Louis also founded schools and colleges. He improved the country roads. He began the great canal which connects the Mediterranean with the Bay of Biscay. He did all in his power to advance the welfare of the kingdom.

At Versailles, a few miles from Paris, he built the largest and most magnificent palace in France. He adorned it with paintings and statues and surrounded it with lovely gardens. There he lived in great splendor, and gathered about him a large company of talented men and beautiful women.

The Louvre, the Trianon, the Tuileries, and some other of the most beautiful buildings for which Paris is still noted were also built during his reign.

In 1660, Louis married Maria Theresa of Spain. A year later, she gave birth to a son, also named Louis. Sadly, although they had five more children, all died young, three in infancy, one at age three, and one at age five.

In 1672, Louis concluded a treaty with his cousin, King Charles II of England, which committed England to supporting France in the conquest of the Netherlands. The subsequent war began with a series of French successes as the large French army quickly over-ran and occupied most of the Dutch provinces. Louis commanded his army in the field in person. But the French invasion stalled at the siege of Amsterdam, and the Dutch flooded their own fields to prevent the French army from maneuvering any further. Eventually, the French were forced to negotiate a treaty of peace in which they agreed to withdraw from the Netherlands.

In 1683, Queen Maria Theresa, age 45, suddenly became ill, and died. Prince Louis, their only surviving child was but twelve years old. The next year, King Louis secretly married one of the ladies at his court, Françoise d'Aubigné Scarron, the Marquise de Maintenon. She became King Louis' closest advisor and all the court seemed to know that in order to get the King's agreement to any proposal, it was necessary to first seek the approval of Madame de Maintenot.

Beginning in 1681, Louis decided to resolve the issue of religion in France by reducing and eliminating the privileges which had been granted to the Huguenots in the Edict of Nantes by his grandfather, King Henry IV. He began insisting that all Protestants must be converted to the Catholic Church. He found an effective means of persuasion when he used his royal prerogative to order Huguenot households to provide lodging for members of the French army, especially for his cavalry troops, known as dragoons. The practice of forcing soldiers to be housed in the homes of Huguenots was called the dragonade. Needless to say, the Huguenots found the practice offensive and often unbearable. If a Huguenot family agreed to convert to Catholicism, they were relieved of the obligation to house troops and any soldiers quartered with them were removed. Sadly these practices were supported by many of the Catholics in France, who resented the continued presence of the Huguenots and considered them disloyal.

In 1685, Louis went a step further and revoked the Edict of Nantes. In consequence over three hundred thousand Protestants left France. They carried with them their tools and their trades and moved into other countries. More than forty thousand of them settled in England, where they were received with open arms. Many came to the English colonies in the New World and were welcomed there as well.

In his later life Louis had the same fondness for war as in his youth. For nearly fifteen years of his reign he was engaged in wars with various European nations. His army was large and thoroughly disciplined. He had also a navy which made France powerful on the ocean. He used to say with great pride, "I can fight the world equally well on the sea or on the land."

Wars were fought with Spain, Holland, England, Germany, and other nations, and brilliant victories were won.

These successes delighted the French people, and they almost adored their "Grand Monarch." Louis XIV became almost as much the terror of Europe as did Napoleon about a hundred years later; and then the decline began.

Among the men who helped to break down the military glory of Louis XIV, was Prince Eugene of Savoy. Prince Eugene was born in Paris, in 1663. As soon as he was old enough for military service he asked King Louis to make him an officer in the French army.

Louis was not friendly to Eugene's mother, and the request of the young prince was refused. Indignant at this, Eugene left France; but he was determined to be a soldier somewhere.

He was twenty years old when the Turks laid siege to Vienna, and he was among the soldiers who helped to drive them back. His bravery brought him into notice, and he rapidly rose from rank to rank in the army of the German Emperor. At twenty-one he was a colonel, at twenty-two a major general, and at twenty-four a lieutenant general. After serving in numerous battles against the Turks, Prince Eugene was sent, in command of an Austrian force, into Northern Italy, where Louis XIV was threatening the province of Savoy.

Eugene now had one of the great satisfactions of his life.

When Louis had refused him a commission in the French army he had said that he would never again enter France except as a conqueror. After several victories in Italy, he marched into France, captured several towns, and returned to Italy laden with great plunder, thus making good his word.

But the most important thing achieved by Eugene and his allies during this war with Louis was the capture of a strongly fortified town called Casal. This town stood near the borders of France and Italy, and commanded the easiest and most frequently traveled pass between the two countries.

When the town was taken, Eugene made it one of the conditions of surrender that its fortifications should be destroyed and never rebuilt. Yet this did not prevent Louis XIV from making other attempts to capture Northern Italy; and Prince Eugene afterwards served in two other long wars that were successfully fought in its defense.

In 1700, King Carlos II of Spain died without any surviving children. In his will, he named one of Louis XIV's grandsons as his heir. The other powers of Europe, the Habsburgs of Austria, and King William III, ruler of England and the Netherlands, feared that this would give France far too much power. Thus began the War of the Spanish Succession. For thirteen years, battles were fought between the forces of Spain and France, united by grandfather Louis XIV, and his grandson, Philip V of Spain on one side and Leopold I, Holy Roman Emperor and first King William III of England and then Queen Anne of England on the other.

Louis thought he could win quickly by sending a French army towards Vienna to defeat Emperor Leopold. But an English army, under the command of John Churchill, the Duke of Marlborough, was able to march rapidly up the Rhine valley and across Bavaria to the Danube where it united with an Austrian army under Prince Eugene. Their combined forces inflicted a decisive defeat on the French army at the Battle of Blenheim.

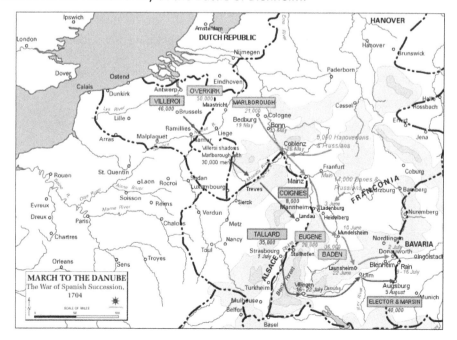

The defeat of Louis XIV, on this occasion, was one of the most disastrous ever suffered by the French. It greatly encouraged those who were defending the liberties of Europe. Louis's power in Bavaria and Holland was shattered, and his armies were never again so much of a terror as they had been. Louis did not, however, give up at once. Fighting continued for about ten years longer; but there were no further victories for France.

When the war was ended, in 1713, by the peace of Utrecht, the French were obliged to give up to the British, Acadia, the Hudson's Bay Territory and Newfoundland. Austria also was given possession of some of the territory which had been held by France.

A year later, in 1714, by the Treaty of Rastatt, it was agreed that all the different nations which had been engaged in the war should have just what belonged to them before the war began.

The glory of France and her "Grand Monarch" had departed. He lived only a little more than two years after peace was proclaimed.

Louis XIV died on September 1, 1715, at the age of seventy-seven, having reigned seventy-two years. His eldest son, Louis (le Grand Dauphin) had died in 1711, at the age of 49. His grandson, Louis, Duke of Burgundy had died in 1712 at the age of 30. Thus, Louis XIV was succeeded by his five-year-old great-grandson, who became King Louis XV of France.

Sources

Catherine de Medici, By Leonie Frieda (2006: Harper Perennial) is a great read, though perhaps too sympathetic to Catherine.

Anne Somerset's biography of Elizabeth (**Elizabeth I**, 2003: Anchor) is the best of the recent works, although Christopher Hibbert's **The Virgin Queen: Elizabeth I (**1992: Da Capo Press) is an interesting read (almost anything by Hibbert is an interesting read!). Antonia Fraser's **King James, VI of Scotland, I of England** (1994: George Weidenfeld & Nicholson) is a good place to start on the Scottish king. I am indebted to my mentor and history teacher from undergraduate days, W.B. Patterson, whose work on James I is rich and nuanced (**King James VI and I and the Reunion of Christendom,** 2000: Cambridge University Press).

The Memory Palace of Matteo Ricci by Jonathan Spence (1985: Penguin) is a delightful, if maddening book. I learned much more about the science of mnenomics than I had time for, searching for the details of Ricci's mission in China.

For those who want the historical background to William Shakespeare, the place to start is **A Year in the Life of William Shakespeare: 1599** (2006: Harper Perennial) by James Shapiro. I also much enjoyed **The Lodger Shakespeare** (2009: Penguin) by Charles Nicholl.

For John Smith, there is no substitute for reading his own memoirs. On the other early colonists, I highly recommend **Champlain's Dream** by David Hackett Fischer (2008: Simon & Schuster), **William Bradford: Plymouth's Faithful Pilgrim** by Gary D. Schmidt (1998: Eerdmans) and **John Winthrop: America's Forgotten Founding Father** by Francis J. Bremer (2005: Oxford University Press). They are each delightful reads and recover a full-featured picture of all three men as Europeans exploring a strange new world.

For King Charles I, there is nothing like the classic work by C.V. Wedgwood's **A Coffin for King Charles** (1964: Penguin). On Cromwell, I will recommend a book long overlooked (unjustly): **Oliver Cromwell** by Theodore Roosevelt (1900: Charles Scribner's Sons). Christopher Hill is his best modern biographer, **God's Englishman: Oliver Cromwell and the English Revolution** (1990:

Penguin). An older biography of **Charles II**, but still worth reading, is the one by Osmund Airy, published in 1901 by Messrs. Goupil & Co.

For **Pascal**, I read and enjoyed the biography by Emile Boutroux, translated by Ellen Margaret Creak (1902: Hachette). I would also highly recommend the young adult biography written by Joyce McPherson (1995: Greenleaf Press)

Simon Schama is an expert on all things Dutch and Rembrandt. His study, **Rembrandt's Eyes** (1999: Knopf) tells the story of the painter, his times, his culture, and many of his contemporary artists. An older, but still excellent study on **Rembrandt** is the one by G. Baldwin Brown (1907: Charles Scribner's Sons).

The Life of John Milton by Barbara Kiefer Lewalski (2002: Wiley-Blackwell) is the best of the modern biographies, but I also enjoyed the **Life of John Milton** by Richard Garnett (1890: Alter Scott). I am much indebted to the Milton Reading Room maintained online at Dartmouth College, edited by Thomas Luxon.

There are excellent online resources for Johannes Vermeer at http://www.essentialvermeer.com, built and maintained by Jonathan Janson and at the http://www.vermeer-foundation.org.

The Life of John Locke by Henry Richard Fox Bourne (1876: Harper & Brothers) is still worth reading for those who want a detailed biography. Bourne's lengthy discourses on Locke's writings are a starting point in analyzing them. The political essays have been much analyzed and commented upon since then, of course.

The Splendid Century: Life in the France of Louis XIV by W.H. Lewis (dedicated to his brother, C.S. Lewis) is still perhaps the best introduction to *le grande monarch*.

All images are from the wiki commons of Wikipedia.com and are in the public domain.